LOUISIANA STATE UNIVERSITY STUDIES

Social Science Series

Rudolf Heberle, Editor

————

Number Four

FREEDOM OF THE PRESS IN THE GERMAN REPUBLIC
1918-1933

LOUISIANA STATE UNIVERSITY STUDIES

Richard J. Russell, General Editor

The Louisiana State University Studies was established to
publish the results of research by faculty members, staff, and
graduate students of the University. Manuscripts of exceptional
merit from sources other than aforementioned are considered
for publication provided they deal with subjects of particular
interest to Louisiana.

The Studies originally appeared as a unified series consisting of forty-two numbers, published between the years 1931 and
1941. In 1951 the Studies was reactivated, and is now being issued
in the following series: Social Sciences, Humanities, Biological
Sciences, and Physical Sciences. Other series may be established
as the need arises.

The Studies in each series will be numbered only serially,
without volume designation.

Requests for exchanges should be addressed to the Gift and
and Exchange Division, Louisiana State University Library,
Baton Rouge. All other communications should be addressed
to the Louisiana State University Press, Baton Rouge.

Freedom of the Press

in the

German Republic

1918-1933

by PETER J. FLIESS

LOUISIANA STATE UNIVERSITY PRESS

Baton Rouge

To the memory of my father.

"Was haben die Deutschen an ihrer scharmanten
Pressfreiheit gehabt? als dass jeder über den
andern so viel Schlechtes und Niederträchtiges
sagen konnte, als ihm beliebte!"

Goethe, August 24, 1809
F. W. Riemer, Mitteilungen über Goethe.

PREFACE

The story of the German press and its freedom in relation to the government of the Weimar republic is revealed less by a series of dramatic events than by the relatively monotonous routine of everyday contacts. Like all phases and facets of history, the experiences of the German press during the period under consideration are of course not lacking in landmarks bringing out in bold relief trends and developments which otherwise could be perceived only with difficulty. Examples are the cases of the Deutsche Allgemeine Zeitung, of Fechenbach, of the Weltbühne and Das Andere Deutschland (all of which are discussed subsequently), as well as such specific events as the waves of assassination and defamation, in which the role of the nationalist press as one of the chief gravediggers of the republic forces itself even upon the most sympathetic observer. However, any exaggerated reliance on such high lights can result in nothing but a distorted picture. A realistic appraisal will have to depend to a greater extent on the plight of the press in its day-to-day relations with the government. Matters such as frequency and length of suppression of newspapers, the nature of administrative and judicial punishment, the degree of intimidation, the motivations of the various agencies of the government have to be ascertained. The dramatic key cases bear upon such questions only tangentially. Unhappily, the necessary information on the day-to-day routine relations between government and press frequently is not available. Much of the obscurity is due to the extensive administrative jurisdiction to which the press was subjected as well as to the federal devolution of authority. However, even judicial decisions in press cases are often shrouded in mystery. Only rarely were such decisions published, and then only in meager excerpts not normally revealing the identity of the newspapers nvolved.

The story of the German press can therefore be gathered only through careful extraction from reliable newspapers, Reichstag debates on interpellations and legislation, texts of laws and decrees, and scholarly discussions. Additional illustrative material could be obtained from the partisan press of the left and of the right. However, their doubtful reliability made it appear inadvisable to include them among the sources for this study. In spite of these methodological difficulties the condition of the press in the Weimar republic is clear and unequivocal. So, equally, is the predicament of the republican government in defending its existence against a subversive press in the face of institutional impediments.

P. J. F.

CONTENTS

ABBREVIATIONS

RGB1 . . . . Reichsgesetzblatt

Sten. Ber. . . . . Stenographische Berichte,
Verhandlungen des Reichstags

StGB . . . . Strafgesetzbuch

CHAPTER I

INTRODUCTION

The Problem of Freedom

One of the most notable results of the two global conflagrations during the first half of the current century has been an extraordinary concern by the victors with the internal political organization of the vanquished. The belief has been widespread that reshaping their former foes in their own liberal image is a first requisite for global restoration. Massive evidence by now has accumulated against the feasibility of grafting the liberal system on a heterogeneous social tree. However, the question as to whether the recurrent failures were due to defects in superstructure or whether their causes were of a more basic nature is of paramount practical importance. Surely, it would be vain for invading armies to erect in the lands of their defeated enemies systems of government based on principles which have conclusively demonstrated their inherently disruptive effects. A survey of the history of the press in the short-lived German republic might add to the illumination of the problem. The issue is, of course, more universal than appears from the present study. Nevertheless, an investigation of this narrow segment of a vast problem may be fruitful. The irreconcilable conflict between individual rights and the legitimate interests of the body politic, as it appears here, reveals a basic social issue in cold, naked realism which may clarify lines difficult to discern where they are blurred by moderation.

The liberal principles written into the constitution of the German republic of 1919 rested, from the very outset, on a fragile basis. The traditional German reverence for governmental authority was not conducive to the perfection of the rights and dignity of the individual. The bitter struggles in which concessions were wrested from the government, creating in England, America, and France a solid foundation for individual rights, were totally lacking in the German tradition. We can only conjecture as to the reasons for this lack of militancy. A more tangible explanation than the vague and elusive concept of national character can no doubt be found. One writer rather convincingly attributes the success of individual liberties in England and America to geographical position which has thus far protected these countries against foreign invasions. Countries not so blessed with the advantages of geography, so the argument runs, were forced to give priority to the attainment of collective freedom from invaders over the liberty of the individual. [1] Perhaps an even more important reason for the success of the individual-rights doctrine in Anglo-Saxon

1

countries has been that sense of participation by the individual in
community affairs which had established an identity of interests
between him and his community long before liberalism was embraced as the theoretical foundation on which political authority
was to rest. Only where such a prior agreement on the primary
interests of society exists among the various groups can the anarchic tendencies of the natural-rights doctrine be tolerated, since
disagreement will then be directed toward secondary issues. In the
absence of this agreement, the state, lest it become the victim of
anarchy, will more frequently be compelled to deny than to concede
constitutional rights, especially where the tradition of toleration is
feeble.

In Germany both liberal tradition and agreement on the basic
social values were lacking when the republic of 1918 was established.
The new political framework was rejected by powerful forces on the
left and on the right. The majority, which supported it at its inception, provided at best a precarious foundation on which to rest
the republican edifice, since fear of communism, rather than genuine
sympathy for the republican form of government, had been the major
driving force. This support could hardly be expected to endure after
the Communists had been forced to abandon their role as serious con-
tenders for political power. Under these conditions, the lack of a
sense of individual participation proved especially disastrous. Sepa-
rated from community affairs, the individual citizen was easily persuaded to assume a position of indifference or even hostility toward
his government once he had become conscious of his theoretical rights
which, by force of necessity, were denied him almost as soon as they
were granted. It was this cleavage between the individual and society
which invited the formation of the nationalist murder organizations in
Germany during the early years of the republic notwithstanding the
relatively pacific political tradition of the country. Once the social
organism had disintegrated into various mutually hostile groups,
there was nothing to prevent a sudden and drastic change of traditional political mores. The formal union, in one political organization, of conflicting groups unwilling to agree even on the most
rudimentary moral and political standard almost inevitably produced
schisms of a revolutionary nature which neither laws nor political
skill could mend.

To rest the protection of human liberties on legal institutions
alone is to lean upon a slender reed. In fact, liberties are nowhere
as much in jeopardy as in the liberal constitutional state if unsupported by tradition and social agreement. The unfitness of liberalism to serve as a universally valid standard without regard to traditional and environmental factors is clearly revealed by the intents
and social conditions surrounding its adoption in countries of the
West. There the earlier constitutional systems were successful in
spite of the essentially empty formalism of liberal constitutions,

which, divorced from the problem of power, were hardly adequate
to the task of reconciling liberty and authority.[2] Their success
can be explained in terms of social conditions accompanying the
adoption of formal constitutionalism by countries of the West at a
time when the industrial mass state still was a thing of the remote
future. The preindustrial nature of society permitted an exaltation
of the individual personality as the ultimate social value from whose
service the state derived its only raison d'être. While liberal constitutionalism has come to be considered as the universal model for
political organization worthy of imitation by all societies, its essence,
however, has been lost in the modern mass state beyond the possibility of recovery. The contemporary tendency toward uniformity,
the subordination of the individual to the collectivity has virtually
signaled the end of individual freedom in mass society. If constitutionalism in the West still demonstrates a tolerable degree of vitality,
this fact is no doubt to be ascribed to the remarkable measure of
social cohesion attained in such countries before the advent of the
mass state.

    In less well-grounded societies there is a real danger that
under the shield of formal liberalism incapable of differentiating
between liberal and antiliberal substance antiliberal forces will
seize power "legally" and then eliminate all vestiges of liberty
through legal means. This threat is accentuated by the fact that
the liberal state, as long as it rests solely on a mechanistic structure, must perforce fill the vacuum arising from the lack of social
cohesion through any means at its disposal. Once that necessity
becomes paramount, there is nothing to prevent the deterioration
of liberalism into totalitarianism. That tendency is aided by the
contemporary dissolution of the social organism of the people
which leaves nothing but an amorphous mass inclined toward anarchy. The state wanting in social basis has then no choice but to
resort to naked force if it is to survive. The inevitable result is
the emergence of an imperialistic leviathan contrived for the
destruction of its subjects. Is it, then, to be wondered at that the
German republic, resting on nothing but a formal liberal foundation
and devoid of traditional substance, was shipwrecked? Was its
failure the result of corruption or political unfitness of its leaders,
or perhaps of the peculiar psychological makeup of the German
people? Or was it the virtually inevitable consequence of a formal
liberalism introduced in times of political and social unrest under
the auspices of a vanquished government? Perhaps the present
examination of the history of the press and its freedom under the
Weimar republic may provide some answers for this general problem.

    The freedom of the press appears an especially appropriate
subject for an investigation of basic rights for two reasons. First,
in the development of modern democracy the press has acquired
new political characteristics. As one of the mediators between the

people and their government, as a channel of information without
which popular participation in public affairs would not be imaginable,
the press is at the same time a private and a public organ. [3] Without such necessary channels, public opinion would be doomed forever
to remain aimless and inarticulate. The opportunity for molding the
amorphous mass of individual opinions into a conscious and purposive
collective opinion is provided primarily by the press. Second, the
freedom of the press, more than any other human liberty, demonstrates the dangers inherent in the adoption of liberal forms which,
devised for past social situations, are inappropriate when applied
to the contemporary world. Whereas free expression was originally
thought to serve the greatest possible approximation to truth and
justice through an exchange of views, parliamentary debate in recent times has been concerned primarily with an adjustment of
interests. Contemporary parties as well as the press serving them,
unperturbed by questions of truth or justice, are almost exclusively
preoccupied with the catching of votes by any available means. [4]
The press has become an important participant in the exploitation
of mass psychology for political as well as for commercial reasons.
Whatever its motivation, sensationalism — made lucrative by the
vast increase in circulation — constitutes a temptation which the
press has found difficult to resist. The political press tries to
attract the greatest possible number of readers to sell its ideology;
the commercial press has the same goal in order to maximize its
profits. Both attempt to attain that end by playing upon the emotions of the masses, yielding, if need be, accuracy of reporting to
sensationalism. A press elevating publicity above truth no longer
performs legitimate journalistic tasks. It has abandoned its primary function of promoting reason for its obfuscation. In failing
to curb such a press, democracy nurtures a monster which may
eventually destroy it. The press therefore cannot be permitted to
use its freedom irresponsibly and place its own pecuniary or ideological interests above those of society. Yet, the formalism of the
freedom of the press has prevented the necessary distinction to be
made between that expression which is devoted to the search for
truth and reason and that which is dedicated to indoctrination through
emotional incitement, propaganda, suppression of reason, and a
general appeal to the base instincts in man. It has precluded an adequate regulation of the means of mass communication by obscuring
their essential difference from conventional means of communication
by individuals. The result has been either an excessive liberality
toward a press which has actually forfeited its freedom, or a swing-
ing of the pendulum to the other extreme of muzzling a responsible
but critical press to the point of preventing it from performing its
proper function. Abundant examples of both can be found in the
relation between government and press in the Weimar republic.

The Press and Parliamentary Paralysis

The justification for a free press as well as its utility presupposes the proper functioning of democratic institutions. Once government renounces popular control, the press can easily be perverted into the tool of an autocratic executive. A number of structural infirmities of the constitutional system enabled the Weimar government to escape accountability to the electorate and its agencies. The defects were not immediately apparent, least of all to the framers of the constitution. Having scrutinized with utmost care the constitutional experiences of other epochs and peoples, the product of their labors was to be a model constitution embedding all the advantages and none of the pitfalls of other constitutions. Yet, in spite of this scholarly approach — or perhaps because of it — the outcome was a hodgepodge of traditional German bias in favor of executive power, a desire for mathematically determinable justice in the system of representation, and a misconceived faith in the techniques of direct democracy. Perhaps the most egregious blunder was the failure to determine with precision the nature and extent of executive responsibility. To call attention to the virtually inevitable usurpation of power in the absence of clearly defined constitutional limitations is to state the obvious. Such was the melancholy fate which befell the German republic. The intent of the framers to follow normal parliamentary procedure by making the chancellor responsible to the Reichstag hardly admits of any doubt. Yet the pertinent constitutional provisions were so formulated as to permit the appointment and dismissal of the chancellor at the discretion of the president. The requirement of parliamentary support for the new chancellor was no practical obstacle to presidential government since a recalcitrant Reichstag could be disabled through dissolution. The period that would elapse between the dissolution and the convening of the newly elected Reichstag was normally of sufficient duration to permit major policy decisions by president and chancellor without parliamentary supervision. Executive discretion was further enhanced by the frequent inability of the Reichstag to produce a majority. This lack of agreement was largely attributable to the electoral system which carried proportional representation to the most absurd extremes. The result was an absolutely staggering number of splinter parties, which frequently were no more than economic pressure groups masquerading under the banner of bona fide political parties. Their number, as well as their reluctance to yield to the requirements of the national welfare, virtually eliminated the possibility of forging a legislative will. Even more disturbing was the emergence during the last years of the republic of a negative majority ever ready to frustrate governmental policy without being able to agree upon a positive policy of its own. Executive government emancipated from parliamentary supervision therefore became a practical necessity if the

republic was to survive. The legal basis for such high-handed procedure was provided by the famous Article 48 which enabled the
president to establish a constitutional dictatorship and suspend most
basic rights in the event of an external or internal threat to the constitutional order. This extraordinary power was surrounded with
constitutional safeguards against abuse, which at first sight seem
quite satisfactory. Emergency decrees issued under this authority
required the countersignature of the chancellor or minister, who was
to be responsible to the Reichstag, and had to be repealed upon legislative request. However, the practical inadequacy of these safeguards
is revealed by the combined authority of the president and the chancellor to proclaim simultaneously emergency decrees and dissolution
of the Reichstag, rendering wholly fatuous any pretense at parliamentary supervision. In this alliance the president was inevitably
the stronger partner, since he could, and did, dismiss and appoint
chancellors without parliamentary consent. This practice was bound
to generate the decay of the republican government if the president
was willing to abandon the path of constitutionalism.

The incorporation of an emergency article in the constitution
was not in itself unorthodox constitutional practice and perhaps was
indispensable in Germany in the light of the conditions accompanying
the establishment of the republic. Yet, to expect that such powers
would always be exercised in the best interest of the constitutional
order is to ignore the facts of political life. Unless surrounded with
rigid safeguards, they constitute a perpetual temptation for rulers to
use them for the permanent elimination of parliamentary restraints.
Article 48 was deficient in leaving the initiative for its invocation to
the beneficiary of the extraordinary grant of power and in failing to
set a time limit for the duration of the constitutional dictatorship.[5]
Without these rudimentary safeguards the already precarious parliamentary supervision was doomed to be ineffective.

The constitutional order was further attenuated by the flexibility
of the amending procedure. The procedure was not used to add specific amendments which would in general supersede the original text
of the constitution. Rather, it was employed to pass legislation which
was in conflict with the constitution. If such legislation had the approval of a two-thirds majority in both houses, it was not subject to the
objection of unconstitutionality, while the constitution itself remained
unchanged. The ease with which the constitution could thus be circum-
vented was a virtual invitation to violate some of the most fundamental
provisions.

Conditions such as these did not bode well for the freedom of
the press. Its potential contributions to public life were apt to be
unwelcome to a government trying, by preference or by necessity,
to escape popular control. Consequently, the need for a free press
as a channel of communication between the public and the government
was minimized by the substitution of less conspicuous but more direct

means of determining the climate of opinion which are at the disposal of an autocratic government.

The Structure of the German Press[6]

While this study is primarily concerned with the relationship between government and press, a more precise idea of the structure of the German press may help to bring the problem into realistic focus. Since its characteristics, however, bear only tangentially on its political condition, they will be stated as concisely as the breadth of the subject will allow. The German press comprised three principal varieties: the government-owned or controlled press, the commercial press (Geschäftspresse), and the so-called ideological press (Gesinnungspresse) reflecting the views of political parties or interest groups. Of the three types the latter is of the most direct concern in the present context because of its wide circulation and direct involvement in the political struggle.

Among the government-owned or controlled newspapers various subcategories are distinguishable. The most directly controlled type was the official government press (offizielle oder Staatszeitung) of which the Deutsche Reichsanzeiger und Preussische Staatsanzeiger is the classical example. This press was normally owned by the government and produced by government-employed editors. Its official part was devoted to official publications of the government, while the unofficial one approximated more closely the character of the nongovernmental press. The government also exercised a measure of control over the semiofficial press (offiziöse Zeitungen). These were political newspapers founded by private entrepreneurs which had become available, through governmental subsidies, for the expression of official views and generally refrained from presenting political opinions of their own. In many respects this press was more useful to the government than the official press. It provided an effective outlet for official views and at the same time enabled the government to influence and arouse public opinion in regard to matters which were not as yet official. It also furnished a forum for governmental polemics which, if printed in the official press, might have provoked domestic and international incidents.

The relationship between the semiofficial press and the government was not always obvious. Occasionally the financial dependence of a newspaper remained latent for some time. Perhaps an even more subtle but equally effective influence was exerted through the official news agencies, which had early come under governmental control.

The most powerful journalistic influence in Germany has been that exerted by the ideological press, which was identified either with political parties or with economic-interest groups. However,

the relationship between press and political party does not present
a uniform picture. Normally party control has been more complete on the extreme wings of the political spectrum and less rigid
toward the center. On the extreme left, the Communist party, which
was generally intolerant of deviations from the official dogma, showed
little inclination to allow its press any latitude whatsoever. Its only
"legitimate" function was the advancement of the Communist cause
through the persuasion of the masses. The Social Democratic party,
though less doctrinaire than the Communists, had equally insisted
from the very beginning on a close connection between party and
press. In contrast to the press of other political parties official
Socialist party organs were permitted little latitude. The attitude
of these papers was determined in theory by their clientele, that is,
the rank and file of the Social Democratic party. In actual practice
this "popular control" was exercised by the hierarchy of the party
organization. Yet, in contrast to the Communist press, an attempt
was made at democratization and the maintenance of a balance between the party bureaucracy and its membership.

A close connection between party and press also characterized
the Catholic Centrist party. However, in contrast to the centralizing tendencies of the Social Democratic press, the Centrist party did
not create a central party organ. Neither of the two prominent Catholic papers, the Germania and Koelnische Volkszeitung, were party
organs in the sense of the official Social Democratic press. Yet,
strong centralizing tendencies were clearly indicated by a number
of financial mergers of Centrist newspapers which severely curtailed
their editorial independence.

The relations between the liberal press and the political parties
whose views it reflected were altogether different. The discipline
arising in the case of the Centrist party from the Church and in the
case of the socialist parties from the organization of the industrial
proletariat was wholly lacking. The reasons were inherent in the
basic individualistic tendencies of liberalism which resists regi-
mentation of any kind. Thus, a party press in the sense of the
Socialist and Centrist organs did not exist. Neither the Democratic
party nor the German People's party, the stalwarts of German
liberalism, had a central organ at its disposal. In fact, a mixture
of partisan views could occasionally be observed in the great papers
which were related through ideological affinities to one of these two
parties. The picture changed during the later years of the republic
when the need for ensuring success forced the Democratic party to
strengthen the organizational bond between it and its press through
the establishment of official and semiofficial news agencies.

The connection of the Nationalist press with the party followed
in essence the pattern of the other middle-class papers. As in the
case of the Democratic and People's parties, a measure of uniformity
of the party press was established through semiofficial news agencies

which would supply the Nationalist press with official views and information.   The press of the National-Socialist party followed rather
closely the pattern of the mass parties of the left.   Rigid in its organizational discipline, it had an official central organ, the Voelkische
Beobachter, to which members of the party in good standing were
expected to subscribe.

Newspapers devoted to the promotion of nonpolitical interests
were in many respects similar to the political press in that they were
designed to convince the general public of the legitimacy of the aims
pursued by them.   Organizations devoted to artistic, scholarly, religious, and economic interests frequently developed extensive publicity apparatuses consisting of newspapers, news agencies, and press
commission.   The greatest and potentially most dangerous influence
upon the daily press was that exerted by economic interests.

As long as the source of information and opinion was overt, the
availability of the press to economic interests was beyond reproach.
However, latent pressures causing it to come to the defense of a particular interest under the pretense of promoting the general welfare
were not without danger.   Moreover, economic interests frequently
did not content themselves with overt press activities.   Through
indirect financial pressures they made an increasing number of newspapers subservient to themselves, restricting journalistic freedom
more severely and effectively than any government has ever succeeded in doing.   Economic fetters were substituted for governmental restraints through the granting and withholding of advertising and credits.

The most powerful economic influences were those exerted by
the banks and heavy industry, who were the first to make systematic
attempts to exploit the press for the promotion of their private interests.   The more potent influence was that exercised by industry
through acquisition of majority stock or financial participation, or
through advertising and acquisition of news agencies.   Its enormous
profits during the war and the subsequent inflation enabled industry
to make the extensive investments required by modern press enterprises.   The investment, which paid generous political dividends,
became especially worthwhile after the revolution of 1918, when the
only way to protect its interest against the government was through
persuasion of the voter.   The acquisition of an increasing number of
newspapers by industry was facilitated by the inflation, which forced
many press enterprises to turn to industry for financial aid.   The
political importance of that press cannot be overstated.   Inherently
sympathetic to the parties of the political right, its defection from
the republic became a matter of open record.   Its political influence
was enhanced by the fact that industrial control was frequently concealed from the readers.   Outstanding examples of industrially controlled newspapers are the Deutsche Allgemeine Zeitung, controlled
by Hugo Stinnes and ideologically close to the German People's party,

and the Nationalist Berliner Lokal-Anzeiger and Der Tag, controlled
by Alfred Hugenberg. To secure an influence on the provincial press
Hugenberg created the Vera Company (Vera Verlagsanstalt G. m. b. H.),
which offered commercial and technical advice and aid to the affiliated
papers. The company succeeded in bringing under its control newspapers which had been especially hard hit economically by the inflation.

Of considerable importance because of its rather wide circulation was the so-called commercial press, which did not have any
overt partisan affiliations. Nevertheless, some basic characteristics were common to both the commercial and the party press. It
should not be assumed that the party press was entirely oblivious of
commercial considerations. Nor would the assumption be justified
that the commercial press was politically neutral and always soli-
citous to avoid taking a stand on political issues. The commercial
press frequently adapted its tenor to the political views of its clientele, which consisted mostly of the middle classes. The only notable
difference between the political and the commercial press was the
latter's nonobservance of a definite party line. Its paramount goal
was the maximization of profits, and its political inclinations were
subordinated to the attainment of that end. Consequently, the commercial press adapted itself to the thought and interests of the ave-
rage citizen, rather than attempt the political persuasion of its
readers. The result was a lack of consistency and frequent oscil-
lations from one political camp to the other.

The financial gains of the commercial press resulting from its
relatively low cost of production and attractiveness for advertisers
because of its high circulation stimulated its development in all
parts of the country. However, they had small appeal to the politically conscious and educated classes who were ideologically committed and whose preference was for the press with a clearly marked
political line. The lack of ideological ties to a political party did not,
however, produce a greater measure of journalistic freedom. On the
contrary, the tendency of the commercial press to become subservient
to all political parties whose membership constituted a potential clientele
deprived it even of that relatively modest measure of independence which
was still retained by the editors of the political press.

CHAPTER II

THE PROBLEM OF INSTITUTIONAL PROTECTION

The inclusion of the freedom of the press in the new German constitution was a foregone conclusion from the very beginning. In fact, only three days after the revolutionary government had been established, the Council of People's Representatives issued a proclamation of the basic principles of government, [1] which included the prohibition of censorship as well as a positive guarantee of free verbal and written expression of opinions. The intention of the government to guarantee the freedom of the press was reaffirmed in the declaration of policy of the new cabinet appointed by President Friedrich Ebert on February 13, 1919. [2] These assurances were merely declaratory, having little if any legal force. They were put on a more solid foundation with the adoption of the constitution of August 11, 1919.

To those who expected of the new government a clear recognition of the press as a political factor indispensable for the proper functioning of a democracy, the new constitution was bound to be disappointing. The freedom to express one's opinions in word and print was guaranteed by Article 118, and censorship was prohibited. Yet, the constitution did not contain any explicit reference to the freedom of the press proper. The inadequacy of the freedom of expression for the protection of the press is apparent. While it shielded editorializing, the reporting of news remained unprotected. It is, of course, perfectly true that the distinction between fact and opinion, editorializing and news reporting, is a tenuous and formalistic one which cannot always be made with precision. A statement of opinion is generally understood to include inferences drawn from facts and an expression of the sentiments aroused by them. Yet, the difference is more apparent than real. Facts have to be selected and formulated, so that it becomes virtually inevitable for opinions to be concealed behind the façade of presumably cold facts. [3] Nevertheless, there was a sufficient difference in degree to exclude news reports from the protection of Article 118. Moreover, there were no defenses against governmental interference with the printing of advertisements, which provides the economic basis for the very life of the press.

The inadequate protection of the press had its historical antecedents. The German constitution of 1849 had guaranteed the freedom of expression without specifically including the press as such. [4] The imperial constitution of 1871 did not contain a bill of rights, apparently because it was felt that the determination of the relations

between man and state was a matter for ordinary, rather than constitutional, legislation. [5] However, the protection of the press in
the constitutions of some of the German states was more satisfactory. [6] It is rather surprising that the tendency of the states to
strengthen the position of the press was not reinforced by the framers
of the Weimar constitution. The apparent incongruity can perhaps
be explained in terms of the failure to appreciate the true significance
of the press for modern democratic society. It was possibly not realized that the function of the press to feed the mass of contemporary
events into the stream of public opinion elevates it to the level of a
semipublic institution endowed with special rights and correlative
obligations. One can merely conjecture regarding the actual motivations of the framers because of the widely divergent views held
by the members of the constitutional assembly. As a matter of fact,
the very adoption of the bill of rights was a matter of considerable
controversy. The delegates of the right were its most ardent pro-
tagonists, [7] whereas the representatives of the moderate left, whose
political philosophy set the general tone for the contents of the constitutional document, were opposed. This is not as startling as it
may appear at first sight. It is not unusual to see the exponents of
conservatism emerge as champions of individual rights in times of
a general shift to the left. As far as the spokesmen of the left were
concerned, their objections were based partly on the conviction that
with the abolition of the absolutist state the protection of individual
rights had lost its raison d'être, [8] and partly on the paramount need
for governmental efficiency required by the precarious external and
internal situation. When Hugo Preuss, the "father" of the Weimar
constitution, cautioned against the immediate adoption of a bill of
rights, he was not motivated by theoretical or ideological considerations but by the realization that the complex subject of a bill of rights
was not conducive to a quick settlement of existing differences and to
easy compromises. [9] However, the general sentiment in favor of a
bill of rights was too strong to be resisted.

The concrete reasons for the omission of a specifically guaranteed freedom of the press are not easy to discern. It has been argued
on good authority that the primary purpose of Article 118 actually was
the protection of the press. [10] As a matter of fact, the corresponding
article had appeared in the constitutional draft under the heading "Freedom of the Press and From Censorship." This phrasing was not, however, taken over into the final text of the constitution, which omitted
all references to the press. The omission suggests that the framers,
though aware of the gap between freedom of the press and of expression, did not desire the inclusion of a comprehensive protection of
the press. Consequently, a wide and vital area of press activities
was left without constitutional defense.

The extent of the freedom of expression itself, as guaranteed by
Article 118, was far from impressive. The fact that it was assured

only "within the limits of the general laws" inspires little confidence
concerning its effectiveness as a substantive restraint upon the government. Perhaps the framers of the constitution had so diligently
studied the theory of democracy as to be wholly unmindful of the
potential dangers to individual liberties which in real life emanated
from the people themselves and their representatives. Thus they
could content themselves with safeguards against the administrative
and judicial branches alone. However, upon closer scrutiny even the
restraints upon these two branches turn out to be an illusion. The
absence of a rigorous separation of powers deprived the term "law"
itself of any precise meaning. The term was not confined to legislative enactments but encompassed police decrees as long as they
served exclusively the maintenance of law and order. [11] Consequently, the freedom of expression under Article 118 was further
stripped of its effectiveness as a guarantee against administrative
encroachments.

The ambiguity of the phrase "general law" precipitated an
endless series of legal arguments which were never really resolved.
It was doubted in some quarters that the framers of the constitution
had actually intended to differentiate between "general laws" and
laws pure and simple. Existing evidence reveals that the constitutional committee had adopted a text which simply provided for the
freedom of expression "within the limits of the laws." By mistake
the attribute "general" slipped again into the version prepared by
the editing subcommittee. [12] Yet, the view that the apparent intent
of the framers robbed the qualification of all practical significance
has little merit in spite of the occasional judicial support of this
interpretation. [13] Surely in case of conflict between intent and
actual wording the latter must prevail lest legal security be wholly
surrendered to judicial discretion. While this was the view of the
majority of German lawyers, the difficulty of defining a general
law remained unresolved. A general law was considered by some
as one which, in contrast to special laws, did not discriminate
against particular opinions. [14] Another view considered general
laws as laws which were not directed specifically against the
expression of opinions but were equally applicable to other rights. [15]
Others still held that general laws were the criminal and tort laws
whereby individuals could be brought to justice for the expression
of opinions violating the criminal laws and the rights of other persons. This interpretation allowed for the suppression of opinions
endangering the maintenance of law and order without, however,
discriminating against any particular opinions or ideologies. [16]

The problem of determining the permissible extent of substantive freedoms compatible with the assertion of governmental
authority is not, of course, peculiarly German. A liberal order in
which freedom is tantamount to license is a self-defeating absurdity.
Liberty without restraint would be the negation of any order and an

open invitation to anarchy, in which all rights save those of the
strong would be denied. Each of the afore-mentioned views doubt-
less has its merits, although none is sufficiently precise to serve
as a satisfactory guide. Obviously the freedom of the press cannot
permit newspapers to place themselves outside the pale of society.
They can reasonably be expected to abide by those general rules of
conduct which apply to all civilized men. Nor is it reasonable to
exempt the press from obligations which individuals and groups in
society are generally compelled to assume. However, the press
may legitimately demand of the government nondiscriminatory
treatment which would preclude the imposition upon some publications, because of the unorthodoxy of their views, of especially
heavy burdens which are not imposed upon more orthodox publications. While it would be patently absurd to extend constitutional
protection to the point of tolerating subversion, the expression of
political views may well be allowed considerable latitude as long
as it refrains from inciting explicitly or implicitly to violence
against the constitutional order. The view of the German Supreme
Court, defining general laws as those which do not prohibit any particular opinion, [17] therefore appears a proper and careful interpretation. Sufficient protection was thereby provided against excessive administrative interference and perhaps, to a more limited
extent, even against legislative abuses. [18] Actually the persistent
concern with inadequate legislative restrictions is somewhat removed from reality in the light of developments during the critical
period preceding the collapse of the German republic, since its
decline was accompanied by executive, rather than legislative,
encroachments of constitutional rights. Constitutional emergency
powers of the executive as well as the far-reaching general powers
of the police, which were outside the pale of constitutional immunities, were the basis for the most formidable encroachments. It is
true, recourse could be had to the ordinary courts against police
measures. However, irreparable harm might have been done to
a publication by the time the aid of judicial agencies could be
solicited.

     While a comprehensive substantive guarantee of the press
was not written into the constitution, Article 118 proclaimed an
explicit prohibition of censorship. This prohibition had the dual
advantage of applying specifically to the press and of avoiding the
inherent ambiguities of substantive freedoms. Yet, even this
clear and simple provision created vexatious problems for German
legal minds. It was by no means clear to them whether censorship
had reference only to preventive control or whether it also embraced
repressive, that is, postpublication measures. There is no doubt
substance in the argument that prepublication censorship is largely
a thing of the past and is resorted to in the contemporary world
only under the most extraordinary circumstances. [19] In fact,

postpublication measures are a far more effective means of control.
The uncertainty and extent of its application introduces an element
of insecurity which inhibits the publisher more than any censor could
do. On the other hand, a broad view of censorship including both
prepublication and postpublication controls would have removed all
possibilities of restraining the press and of holding it to its responsibilities. The general consensus of opinion of the lawyers was
therefore that the framers merely had had preventive censorship in
mind. [20] However, in spite of this far-reaching consensus not all
difficulties of meaning were removed. The general uncertainty is
reflected by the lack of uniformity of police action. After the constitution had come into force some local police authorities, for example,
ceased to enforce the regulations of the Trade Code[21] which provided
that literary products offered for sale by itinerant salesmen be submitted to police authorities for attestation of their moral and religious
propriety. Others continued the old practice, the constitutional prohibition of censorship notwithstanding. The courts upheld the latter
view by drawing a distinction between prepublication examination of
printed matter as such and the necessity of obtaining previous permission for one particular mode of distribution.[22] There can be
little doubt that these interpretations enabled the police to suppress
unwelcome newspapers and periodicals sold in the streets or through
subscription. Thus judicial interpretation robbed the only specific
and definite protection of the freedom of the press of much of its
effectiveness.

The precarious status of the press under the Weimar constitution is evident, although a limited sphere of its activities did
enjoy constitutional protection. To evaluate accurately the effectiveness of that limited protection, it will be necessary to gain some
clarity regarding the actual significance of the fundamental rights of
the Weimar constitution in general. The question inevitably arises
as to whether basic rights were immediately binding positive norms
or merely declaratory of a policy yet to be enacted. In the absence
of any definite clues given by the constitution or its framers we can
merely conjecture. In the light of historical tradition it appears
that the immediate legal validity of constitutional rights, so characteristic of American practice and prevalent in Germany before 1848,
long since had been abolished. The tendency to disparage individual
rights was no doubt reinforced by the general growth in the contemporary world of antiliberal tendencies condoning increasingly encroachments by the state. The judicial inclination in Germany to
deny binding force to these rights surely did not bode well for the
effectiveness of the bill of rights; nor was Hugo Preuss's admission
that the character of each specific right had to be established from
case to case[23] in any way reassuring. What is more important,
however, is that the German legal tradition itself would discountenance a generous view of the legal significance of basic rights.[24]

The paramount importance of tradition for the functioning of a liberal system is clearly demonstrated by the virtual impossibility of effectuating substantive rights through mere formalities devoid of content. Therefore the question is of some relevance whether the general climate of opinion favored a view of basic rights as presocial and prelegal rights of man based on the law of nature or whether they were regarded as derivatives of the positive politico-legal order. The general German view was associated with the traditional conception of the constitutional state (Rechtsstaat) which implied effective limitations of executive and judicial powers. The legislative power, on the other hand, was conceded unbounded liberty. As long as the latter proceeded im Rechtswege, that is, observed the formal requirements for legislative procedure, it was at liberty to enact any rules that appeared expedient. [25] Only rarely could a voice be heard insisting on subordination of the legislative power to suprapositive norms. [26] This view derives in part from the positivist and historicist schools of jurisprudence which dominated German legal thought during the nineteenth century. In part it was undoubtedly caused by the logical contradiction between the political creeds of democracy, which always has a connotation of majority rule, and of liberalism with its emphasis on the inviolability of the individual. As a result, there has developed among the German adherents of the democratic creed an attitude neglectful of the desirability of an effective separation of powers, which has been characterized as "democratic Rousseauism." [27] The need to resolve the incompatibility between the precepts of radical democracy and the natural-rights doctrine was ignored by the framers of the constitution. In view of this tradition and the general hostility which confronted the young republic, it is little wonder that the integration of the individual into society should have been tantamount to his unqualified subordination to its interests. In fact, the paramountcy of the state was hardly ever questioned. [28] No doubt the problem of reconciling the need for stability with the anarchic implications of the natural-rights doctrine should have been a frightening prospect even to more experienced democratic politicians and statesmen. A further difficulty was posed by the value neutrality of basic rights applicable even to those bent upon their destruction. The commitment of a liberal democracy to respect basic human rights renders it easy prey to its enemies in time of emergency. In the Weimar republic this general dilemma was accentuated by the vacillating attitude of its fathers. The disparagement of the republic in the eyes of the people was the virtually inevitable result.

On the institutional side the effectiveness of fundamental rights suffered greatly from the failure to establish a well-defined separation of powers. The laxity in differentiating between the various functions of government is well illustrated by the inclusive manner with which the term "law" in the sense of Article 118 was used. It did not allow for a precise distinction between legislative and execu-

tive functions. Constituting an even more flagrant violation of the
principle were the provisions of the famous emergency Article 48,
which has been discussed in the preceding chapter, [29] and the laxity
of their interpretation. The invocation of the emergency situation
was not reviewable by the courts, which refused to assume jurisdiction over what they considered an acte politique. They would
interfere only in the event of an excès de pouvoir. [30]

The foregoing analysis reveals a rather unimpressive picture
of the protection afforded the press by the constitution. Fundamental
rights generally did not have indisputable immediate validity. For
all practical purposes, they were at the mercy of unabated legislative
discretion. The substantive freedom of the press under Article 118
itself was faulty and incomplete and failed to include a considerable
range of rudimentary press activities. The only direct and immediately enforcible protection of the press as such, the prohibition of
censorship was greatly constricted through judicial interpretation.
Moreover, timidity on the part of the framers to commit themselves
to a clear-cut natural-rights doctrine is unmistakable. Heirs of the
tradition of legal positivism, they must have thought of any appeal
to natural law and natural right as an arrant absurdity. Their reluctance was probably reinforced by the anticipation of difficulties
which the young republic would have to face. The result was a rather
tepid bill ot rights hedged in by many qualifications which in the last
analysis would ensure the primacy of the state over the individual.
A timid liberalism such as this — which in the absence of a liberal
tradition represented perhaps the attainable optimum — could not
bode well for the effectiveness of basic rights, nor was it apt to
impress a nation inexperienced in liberal democracy with the latter's
blessings. It is, of course, perfectly true that the institutional protection of substantive rights is problematical even under optimum
conditions. In contrast to procedural guarantees, substantive rights
admit of no possibility to apply a precise objective standard. Their
dependence on the continuous and fluid process of balancing liberty
and authority inevitably leaves a measure of discretion in drawing
the line between permissible and nonpermissible freedom of expression in each individual case. Consequently, the legitimate sphere
of freedom will vary with time and place, and their institutional
protection will of necessity rest on a tenuous foundation. In the last
analysis, its most secure support is the spirit of toleration prevailing in society. The traditional factor thus assumes increasing importance, and the possibility of developing such a spirit has little promise in a situation such as that which accompanied the birth and
early years of the Weimar republic. However, if an attempt to
establish such a system was to be made nonetheless, an unqualified
and courageous commitment was imperative. Limitations of the
freedoms, which were inevitable in real life, could well have been
left to the judiciary.

In spite of the sincere attempts to liberalize German government, the conclusion is inescapable that the scope of the constitutional
freedom of the press was not in essence enlarged beyond what it had
been under the imperial government. The imperial constitution did
not contain guarantees of the freedom of the press; the matter was
left to ordinary legislation. The Press Law of 1874[31] did not refer
to the substantive rights of the press but, within its narrow limits,
provided rather effective procedural safeguards. It consisted of
regulations concerning the physical make-up of the press, duties
and responsibilities of those connected with its production and distribution, as well as the nature of permissible sanctions. This
law was not abrogated by the framers of the constitution, nor was
it considered incompatible with the provisions of the constitution.[32]
It was actually this carry-over from imperial Germany, rather than
the new republican constitution, which circumscribed the relationship between state and press with some degree of accuracy. In
contrast to the constitutional provisions, the Press Law dealt specifically with the freedom of the press. Its purpose was to impose
upon the government restraints of a procedural nature. It did not
define the freedom of the press in the substantive sense. Rather,
it was in essence a police law protecting the press against police
and administrative, however not against legislative, action.[33]
It removed the press somewhat from the authority of the police.
While the general police laws conferred general authority upon the
police to prevent criminal offenses and maintain public safety and
order,[34] the press was partially immune against such broad preventive measures. For example, the distribution of printed matter
of punishable content could not be prevented by the police, except
in accordance with the very exacting requirements of the Press Law.
Otherwise the police was forced to rely on judicial remedies.[35]
The Press Law, although it was merely a legislative act which
could be superseded by ordinary legislation, provided in some
respects a far more effective protection than the constitution,
since it was not afflicted with the congenital ambiguities of the
latter.

The provisions of the law were partly of a regulatory nature
prescribing the make-up of the press and requiring that publisher
and responsible editor be named in each issue of a newspaper. A
copy of every issue was to be deposited with the police authorities
simultaneously with distribution, however, not for purposes of
prepublication control. It protected individuals and the government against inaccurate or false reporting by compelling the press
to make corrections (Berichtigungszwang). The underlying purpose obviously was the prevention of abuses of the freedom of the
press. It was felt that the truth, which was expected to emerge
through such corrections, was a matter of public concern. In
true Miltonian fashion the victory of truth in the free contest of

conflicting facts and opinions was anticipated with more confidence
than is warranted by a sober evaluation of human experience. The
fact that the "right to correct" may be used for the propagation of
untrue as well as of true information was somewhat naively ignored. [36]
While these regulatory provisions may not have been conducive to the
development of a free press, they certainly did not prevent the press
from a free exercise of its legitimate function.

Another sphere regulated by the Press Law was that of criminal
acts committed through the press. Reaffirming the validity of general
criminal legislation for the press, the locus of accountability for violations was determined. All persons connected with the production and
distribution were criminally liable from the publisher through the
author down to the printer and distributor. No doubt an unfair burden
was thereby put on those who were not normally in a position to judge,
and not necessarily interested in, the contents of what they were pro-
ducing and distributing. [37] The absurdity of this provision and its
detrimental effects upon the freedom of the press were evidently
recognized by the Supreme Court when it decided that it would be a
judicial error to impose generally and indiscriminately on every
printer the duty to check the contents of all the products of his printing press as to their possible criminality. [38] The legal uncertainty
created by this provision is difficult to overemphasize. The same
newspaper or periodical might be confiscated by one court, released
by another, destroyed by one, and declared inoffensive by another
court as a result of the accountability of the many different agents
participating in production and distribution. Whenever an objectionable newspaper was distributed, the very act of distribution constituted a distinct and independent delict. If one single copy happened
to get to a given place, all those connected with its production and
distribution could be held responsible in that place. [39]

More problematical than the regulatory provisions were those
which dealt with confiscation of newspapers and periodicals by police
authorities. Confiscation without judicial authorization was permitted
in the event of violation of the regulatory provisions or of criminal
laws designed to secure social and governmental stability in case of
an external or internal threat. The same authority, with minor
qualifications, extended to instances of vilification of the sovereign
(Majestätsbeleidigung); public incitement to criminal activities;
incitement to class struggle; and the distribution, production, and
advertising of indecent publications. The threat to the freedom of
the press inherent in such confiscations is too apparent to be denied.
The press is especially vulnerable to this type of repression, since
its appeal depends on the news value of its reports. Consequently,
the confiscation of a newspaper for only a few days may have disastrous long-range effects. Even if confiscated papers are released
quickly, their value, which depends on quick distribution to the reader,
has been greatly impaired, and frequent confiscation of the same paper

in short intervals may lead to its total economic destruction. The temptation for the police to abuse such a general authority is at times irresistible. Police authorities everywhere have a congenital tendency to take a broad view of their powers. They are easily persuaded to proceed against newspapers on the basis of generally critical attitudes toward the government. However, once the police is in a position to silence a critical press, all pretense of freedom of the press becomes illusory. The dilemma of the press is by no means hypothetical or imaginary. Mobility and rapidity of distribution undeniably requires expeditious police action in the event of acute danger. Prerequisite judicial authorization cannot be permitted to prevent effective police action. The Press Law therefore did not immunize the press entirely against confiscation by police authorities, but merely placed it in a privileged position which was one step removed from the broad general power of the police. [40] Police action could be taken against the press only in situations of extreme political urgency specified in the Press Law. The press was further protected by the requirement of judicial confirmation of confiscations within a short period of time. The prescribed time limits, which were frequently difficult to observe, were designed as a discouragement to rash action by the police and an ensurance that confiscation would be resorted to only as a very exceptional device in especially critical situations. [41]

If the Press Law afforded protection only against administrative encroachments by the federal government, its prohibition on state governments extended further in that it immunized the press against action by legislatures as well. The protection did not, of course, extend to all state legislation but merely to press laws. In other words, it remained subject to all general state laws which were not directed at the press as such. [42]

There can be little doubt that the German press found its most effective and institutionally tangible protection in the old imperial Press Law. This is not perhaps too surprising in that this law was of a strictly procedural nature and did not touch upon the substantive freedom of the press. It is only in the latter that the maintenance of the delicate balance between liberty and authority becomes problematical. In contrast, procedural guarantees apply equally to all cases regardless of content. All subjective considerations are excluded. Also, unlike the constitution, it protected the freedom of the press as such and not merely the freedom of expression. Even if one makes allowance for the fact that the Press Law was a legislative norm subject to repeal at any time by a simple legislative majority, it still does not compare unfavorably with the constitutional protection. It will be recalled that constitutional liberties were largely vitiated by the "general laws" clause and its broad judicial interpretation as well as by the possibility of suspension under Article 48, which was frequently practiced during the life span of the republic. It is therefore doubtful whether the constitutional liberties had even as much practical significance as the Press Law. While the prohibitions of the Press Law stood until a legislative majority was willing to change them, constitutional provisions rested on a far more tenuous foundation.

The Press Law, which in essence was an old-fashioned police law aiming to restrain administrative discretion, was, however, ill-designed to cope with the most acute menace to the press. It was totally negligent of the fact that the modern democratic press is not so much threatened by administrative agencies as by representative assemblies and antidemocratic judiciaries. Thus, its failure to concern itself with the substantive freedom of the press and its overemphasis on the criminal liability of those connected with its production constituted very serious defects and detracted substantially from its usefulness. The Weimar constitution did nothing to remedy these shortcomings. Nor did it strengthen the position of the press beyond the situation created by the Press Law of 1874. At first sight, it may seem somewhat startling that the imperial government, which can hardly be suspected of much liberality, rather than the republic should have afforded the press its only effective protection. However, this seeming generosity will appear less mysterious if one realizes that the Press Law served the dual purpose of protecting the press, on the one hand, and, on the other, of defending the imperial government against the dangers of an unrestrained press, should the growing pressure of liberal tendencies eventually make radical demands. [43]

Mention should be made of one provision of the general penal code, since it clearly reveals the difficult position of the press in Germany. This provision (Section 193, StGB) stipulated that libelous statements made to protect legitimate interests of the person making them (zur Wahrnehmung berechtigter Interessen) were punishable only insofar as the libel was contained in the form of the utterance proper. Since the law was singularly uninformative regarding the extension of such privileges to the press, the question was left entirely to judicial interpretation. [44] The judiciary took the view that the press, if it became involved in a libel suit, was not entitled to the status of an agency legitimately protecting the interests of the public. Therefore the protection of Section 193 was denied to those responsible for the contents of newspapers and periodicals. [45] It was conceded only if the editor had expressis verbis received a mandate to represent them from the parties having a legitimate interest. The press could not automatically be assumed to stand in an agency relationship to its subscribers or readers in general. [46] Even if a newspaper was closely identified with a political party, its refutation of an attack against the affiliated political party would not invoke the privileges of Section 193 unless the attack had also been made on persons responsible for the paper. [47] The press was considered entitled to criticize corruption if such criticism entailed no insult to individuals responsible for it. [48] The attitude of the courts of law reflects their misconception of the potentially useful and legitimate

contribution of the press to the operation of contemporary democracy. The possibility of a free democratic press was thereby
severely handicapped from the outset.

The reluctance of the courts to concede to the press its right-
ful place as an agent and "advocate" of the public is well illustrated
by the following cases. In one case a newspaper affiliated with a
political party had accused, in the course of an election campaign,
the administration of a municipality in Thuringia of graft. The court
denied that the editor, since he was not a resident of the municipality
involved, could plead mitigating circumstances of legitimate interests
as an agent of a particular public. The only reason for his eventual
acquittal was the fact that he represented a coalition of middle-of-
the-road parties which had given him an express and specific mandate to advocate their cause. In a further decision the Bayerische
Oberlandesgericht made it quite clear that political parties and
political interests were not entitled to the special consideration
which Section 193 permitted. A Socialist paper agitating for the
protection of minor girls in industrial occupations was not thought
to be acting in the defense of legitimate interests. These were
matters which, in the view of the court, did not concern the editor
personally. That they constituted legitimate concerns of the political party with which his newspaper was affiliated was not held
sufficient ground for the extension of the benefits of Section 193.

The views of the courts changed somewhat in the 1920's. The
impetus may well have been provided by a draft criminal code recog-
nizing the representation of the public interest as a legitimate function
of the press which was under consideration by the Reichstag. [49]
Although this code was never adopted, it did not remain entirely
without effect upon the courts. The principle was given limited
recognition by the Supreme Court in a decision of January 20, 1928,
conceding editors of newspapers a legitimacy of interests if they had
received a specific mandate from the parties whose interests were
affected. [50]

This, in rough outline, was the institutional framework within
which the press was to function under the Weimar republic. Its
effectiveness, as has been indicated, to provide a secure area of
freedom for journalistic operations was not impressive. The basic
reason is twofold. The expectation that institutional forms could
divert the course of tradition or compensate for traditional omissions
was unreasonable and stands in direct repudiation of historical experience. In fact, it is no exaggeration to state that the failure of
the framers to approximate the requisite institutional scheme was
not alone responsible. The genesis of the constitution as well as the
final product clearly demonstrates that the framers themselves were
tinged with more than a judicious skepticism toward the principles
which they were now attempting to translate into constitutional reality.
However, their inability to conquer their own traditional bias was
probably secondary in importance to the inherent impossibility of
the task they set out to perform.

CHAPTER III

THE PRESS AND POLITICAL INSTABILITY
1918 - 1923

The difficulty of securing the freedom of the press in a context devoid of liberal tradition is amply illustrated by the plight of newspapers during various periods of the Weimar republic. Each of these periods presents a different major problem in the relationship between government and press and points up clearly the general causes which were responsible for the latter's insecurity. The life span of the republic can be conveniently divided into three distinct periods. First came the time of the consolidation of the republic, from 1918 until the end of the early civil strife in 1923. During these years the young republic had to defend itself against the violent attacks of both the left and the right, and the overriding need for political stability could permit only little scope to the freedom of the press. These early struggles were followed by a period of relative stability and prosperity which lasted until the first signs of the world economic crisis appeared on the horizon in 1929. These were years of a seeming acquiescence of the Germans in the republican government and the integration of Germany into the international community. The government appeared sufficiently entrenched to permit the press a wide latitude. However, even during these peaceful and prosperous years the lack of a liberal tradition prevented the free operation of the press. A systematic fight against the republic was carried on by a conservative civil service and judiciary whose actions were designed to reduce the constitution to a mere sham. In the third period the early impact of the world economic crisis which was felt between 1929 and 1932 resulted in growing discontent in Germany and precipitated the growth of an increasingly intransigent nationalism which tended to discredit the republican ideals in the eyes of the people. This tendency was supported by the generally assumed responsibility of the republic for the signing of the Treaty of Versailles and the subsequent loss of Germany's international prestige. The lack of economic stability accompanied by considerable political insecurity again prevented a comprehensive freedom of the press. This briefly is the framework for the present discussion of the relationship between government and press.

During the early period, in which the new government attempted to consolidate its position, the republic oscillated between the political extremes from which support was alternately expected. Throughout these first five years, the republic was engaged in a two-front war in which it alternately enlisted the aid of one political extreme against

the attacks of the other. The success of that strategy seems indicated by the survival of the republic during its infancy. It succumbed
only when, toward the end of its life span, it had to fight both fronts
simultaneously and its opponents abandoned force in favor of more
subtle methods.

The War Against the Left

Contrary to all expectations, the most active opposition during
the first two years of the republic did not emanate from the traditional opponents of republicanism. In fact, it was not until the
spring of 1920 that the right attempted to overthrow the new form
of government. The reasons for the initial docility of the antirepublican forces of the right are not difficult to discern. During
the early years the restoration of the monarchy was not considered
a practical possibility. Since the right was still stunned by the
events leading to the revolution, it was not at all certain whether
it would be able to muster sizable public support. Strangely enough,
it was the schism within the victorious left which endangered the
survival of the republic from the very beginning. The existing disagreements within the leftist camp revolved around Socialist aims
and methods, interpretations of democracy, and systems of representation. While both majority Socialists (Sozialdemokratische
Partei Deutschlands) and minority socialists (Unabhängige Sozialdemokratische Partei Deutschlands) were in agreement on the
rejection of revolutionary methods, they differed sharply regarding
the system of representation. The majority wing favored the parliamentary system, while the independents advocated the council,
or soviet, system. The two parties, in turn, were split within
themselves. The result was, on the one hand, an eventual rapprochement between the left wing of the SPD and the right wing of
the USPD and, on the other, of the left wing of the USPD and the
"Spartacus Bund,"[1] which later became the nucleus of the as yet
nonexistent Communist party (Kommunistische Partei Deutschlands).
This alignment eventually led to party mergers in 1920 and 1922 respectively. The Independent Socialist party disappeared in the process and the Communist party was formed.[2] Attempts to mend the
schism between majority and minority Socialists initially seemed successful. Both factions were represented in the Council of People's
Representatives which functioned as an interim cabinet in the
period between the disappearance of the imperial government
and the first general elections. However, when the final decision
concerning elections for a National Assembly was in favor of the
parliamentary system, the minority Socialists withdrew from the
temporary government.[3] The tension between the hostile Socialist factions gained in intensity when the majority Socialists, in

their struggle against radical Socialist elements, [4] began to rely
heavily on the support of the former imperial high command. The
hostility grew more intense in the early days of January, 1919. The
disturbances provoked by the discontented Spartacists were falsely
interpreted by the majority socialists as an open challenge to their
authority. The rebellion was squelched through the collaboration
of such heterogeneous elements as Socialist workers, former sol-
diers, and units of counterrevolutionary volunteers commanded by
former officers of the imperial army. The latter were glad to
seize the opportunity to mitigate prevalent leftist tendencies by
combating Socialist workers under the command and responsibility
of majority Socialists. [5] In the subsequent unrest in various parts
of the Reich emanating from the extreme left, the majority Socialists came to rely increasingly on the counterrevolutionaries. The
growth and activities of these groups, organized in so-called "Free
Corps," are probably one of the most sordid episodes in the history
of the Weimar republic. [6] There can be little doubt that from a long-
range point of view the Socialist reliance on antirepublican and
counterrevolutionary forces was an egregious blunder. The frequent
employment of these irregular units resulted in the total disarma-
ment of Socialist workers, who might have been useful later in the
defense of the republic had they been permitted to retain their
striking power. The impotence of the government in controlling
the Free Corps was soon apparent. The frequent excesses committed by them could not be prosecuted with much vigor. Since
neither civil service nor judiciary had been purged in the course of
the revolution, rightists guilty of political crimes, if at all brought
to justice, were generally assured of leniency and sometimes even
aided by their prosecutors to escape. This tendency toward lenient
treatment was even more pronounced in the case of army personnel,
since the government had extended the privilege to the military
forces to try their own personnel by courts-martial even for
civilian offenses. [7]

During the year 1919 the Free Corps, under the command of
the majority Socialist government in Berlin, were employed against
striking Socialists in Central Germany. In Bavaria, they were to
stamp out the soviet republic which had been formed following the
assassination of the Independent Socialist prime minister, Kurt
Eisner, by a young Nationalist student. Furthermore, they gained
in influence and strength by maintaining a protracted state of siege
which seemed to become a perpetual condition throughout the
Reich. [8]

The events of this early period boded ill for the realization of
the lofty liberal principles which had been repeatedly proclaimed,
first by the Council of People's Representatives, then by the
Scheidemann cabinet, and which were finally incorporated into
the constitution itself. The need for sustained military measures

provoked by the disturbances of the left, seriously obstructed the
free operation of the oppositional press in spite of the principles
proclaimed. While censorship was not invoked, the press was
subject to numerous warnings and suppressions strongly reminis-
cent of the period before 1848.[9] Thus, for example, the Rote
Fahne, central organ of the Communist movement, was suppressed
for nearly an entire year in connection with the prohibition of the
Communist party in the spring of 1919 following its instigation of
the general strike in Central Germany.[10] Understandably the defense effort of the republic during the early years was directed
exclusively against the extreme left, which presented the only
acute threat to its survival. No open rebellion had as yet been
attempted by the right, which was satisfied, for the time being,
to exploit the general insecurity for the more immediate purpose
of reducing the strength of the extremist workers.[11]

Measures against the leftist press became even more stringent
as a result of the events that came to pass later the same year. The
old struggle between the proponents of the parliamentary and of the
soviet systems of representation continued after the National Assembly had been elected. A constitutional compromise had been
reached which guaranteed workers' participation in industrial
management and held out the promise of eventual socialization
of industry. However, a bill introduced in the National Assembly
to implement these provisions proved disappointing to extreme
leftists, and a demonstration was staged with the permission of
the Berlin chief of police, a majority Socialist. When some of
the demonstrators disarmed and maltreated several police officers
and eventually prepared an attack against the Assembly building,
the police opened up machine-gun fire. The general leftist dissatisfaction with the workers' council law (Betriebsrätegesetz)
which was eventually enacted provoked widespread strikes in most
industrial areas of the Reich. The strike wave was preceded by a
proclamation of the Communist party, published in the Rote Fahne,
inciting workers to substitute revolutionary councils for capitalist
control of industrial production.[12] To check the strike wave, emergency measures were invoked by the president of the Reich on the
basis of the constitutional emergency article (Article 48), temporarily suspending the free-speech article of the constitution and prohibiting oral and printed expression designed to imperil the proper
functioning of public carriers and utilities.[13] The proclamation
of this measure was followed by wholesale suppression of Independent Socialist and Communist party newspapers.[14] Moreover,
the decree affected retroactively articles published well before its
proclamation. The action of the government was justified by the
chancellor, Gustav Bauer, in the session of the Reichstag of
January 13, on the grounds that the Independent Socialist party
had tried to surrender the parliament, elected on the basis of the

most liberal electoral law in the world, to the dictatorship of the mob. [15] The Prussian minister of the interior, Wolfgang Heine, added that to maintain law and order he had no alternative but to resort to extraordinary measures. [16]

The unusual severity and arbitrariness with which restrictive and punitive measures were imposed called forth a protest of the Association of Metropolitan Newspaper Publishers, which objected to suppressions without indication of reasons and time limit and denying the right of appeal to the courts of justice. It was contended that the measures, imposed without judicial proceedings, were tantamount to economic destruction of publishers and editors as well as of the technical personnel. [17] The legitimacy of these complaints seems borne out by the fact that as moderate a paper as the Berliner Tageblatt demanded in strong terms that the republican government concede at least such guarantees as had been granted by previous military regimes. [18] In response to such protests, the government reaffirmed the principle of the freedom of the press, but accused the leftist press of having abandoned the traditional methods of the political struggle for incitements to violence. Preventive measures were justified in terms of the government's paramount duty to maintain law and order. [19] The danger inherent in that view is apparent considering the high sensitivity of the press to repression. Suppression even for a limited period therefore should not have been the exclusive prerogative of the executive branch, especially since in the event of a serious offense against public safety a speedy court trial easily could be obtained.

A remedy was eventually provided through the establishment of a committee of the Reichsrat[20] to review appeals against prohibitions of newspapers and periodicals. Although the creation of this committee undoubtedly had a remedial effect by curbing governmental excès de pouvoir, it could not cope with the damage caused by the unrestrained issuance of prohibitions which, even if only of short duration, frequently inflicted irreparable losses upon the publications affected. The committee did not function long enough to permit an evaluation of its effectiveness. Its establishment was followed almost immediately by an open rebellion by the right which required the adoption of new and different methods of defense.

The Two-Front War
Strategy of Defamation: Erzberger and Ebert

When early in 1920 the immediate danger of a seizure of power by the extreme left seemed to have been averted, the right launched its first open attack upon the new system of government. In this endeavor it employed most effectively the strategy of defamation against the personal integrity of individuals prominently identified with the political life of the republic. [21] This strategy was a radical departure from the methods employed by the left. The latter had appealed openly to their followers to prepare for the forcible over- throw of the "capitalist system." While the repression of a move- ment inciting to open violence does not pose any great difficulties, the government was far more vulnerable to the subtle and more effective strategy of defamation directed against its leading per- sonalities. This method served the dual purpose of discrediting the republican system in the eyes of the people and of intimidating its leaders. Defamatory campaigns, systematically conducted by the press of the extreme right, frequently provoked political assas- sinations during the early years of the republic. The first assassina- tions could no doubt be credited to emotions aroused by the lost war and the revolution. However, beginning with the year 1920, the problem assumed more serious proportions. Systematic repetitions, in inflammatory language, of mostly unfounded accusations against public personalities created an atmosphere conducive to the resort to violence in the political struggle. The wave of political murders was ushered in with the first unsuccessful attempt on the life of Matthias Erzberger, then Reich minister of finance. The would-be assassin, when questioned, described his prospective victim as a parasite who had to be exterminated and admitted that his action was based on information he had read in the press day after day. The newspaper involved was one closely identified with the extreme right, which in stirring terms had denounced Erzberger, the number one scapegoat for the national frustrations associated with the "shame of Versailles." The attempted murder, acclaimed by the Nationalist press as a patriotic and heroic deed, [22] was celebrated by some Nationalist organizations as a victory of the Nationalist cause. [23] The government clearly perceived the serious implications of such encomiums for the security of the republic. However, the remedial effect of drastic measures such as the suppression of newspapers that had attacked leading political personalities was far from unequi- vocal. It was quite possible, if not probable, that the reverberations would be the reverse of the intended consequences. Nevertheless, the need for stringent measures against the press appeared so over- whelming that a disregard of such caution as political sagacity might have dictated under less pressing conditions seemed justified. [24]

The courts were not without blame in promoting political vio- lence. Their leniency toward persons guilty of defamation was bound to act as an encouragement rather than as a deterrent. A case in point are the libel suits brought by Erzberger and Ebert, which oc- casioned severe attacks by the press. In the suit brought by Erz- berger against the editor of the Kreuzzeitung the court quite properly objected to such statements as: "Erzberger is a cancerous growth";

"I express my contempt for him publicly"; "He is a coward"; and
"He occupies a ministerial post to the detriment of Germany." It
took a similar stand toward assertions that Erzberger combined
political activities with business, that he was not truthful, and
that his political activities were harmful to Germany. Yet, the
offender was merely fined 300 marks, and the libelous articles
ordered confiscated and destroyed. [25] The leniency of the sentence
was explained by the court in terms of the editor's patriotic motivations. [26] The incident occasioned an expression of gratitude to the
Kreuzzeitung by the Nationalist Berliner Lokal-Anzeiger for a job
well-done which deserved the eternal gratitude of the German
people. [27] Shortly before the Erzberger case, the president of
the Reich, Ebert, had sued the rightist Deutsche Zeitung, which
had accused him of a lack of honor and dignity because of his consent to the signing of the Treaty of Versailles. The court objected
to the language used by the newspaper and fined the editor 300 marks. [28]

These two cases, especially the Erzberger case, illustrate the
inadequacy of the libel suit as a defense against the subversive strategy of the right. In fact, the trials provided the Nationalists with
a forum from which they could launch their attacks upon the republic all the more effectively. Even if convicted, the defendant
would frequently emerge victorious, since the trial provided him
with an opportunity to produce evidence which, though unsatisfactory
to the courts of law, might satisfy the court of public opinion. To
deny the lasting effects of such smear campaigns, no matter how
ill-founded the accusations, is to ignore the realities of political
life. Moreover, the court itself cannot be wholly absolved of the
charge of letting itself be swayed by an antirepublican bias in the
Erzberger case. Mistaking radical politics of the right for patriotism, it recognized extenuating circumstances in favor of
the defendant, who presumably had been motivated by patriotic
sentiments. Similar concessions were rarely, if ever, made to
offenders identified with the extreme left, even when they were
motivated by the interests of a far greater number of Germans
than the right.

After the attempt on Erzberger's life, it was still the left
that had to bear the brunt of governmental repression. Confiscations
and suppressions of the rightist press continued to be rare occurrences. To explain this apparently incongruous phenomenon one
does not have to drift far afield. The Communist charges that the
Social Democrats had hedged a sinister plot with the counterrevolutionaries for the extermination of the extreme left seem farfetched.
Rather, the reasons were clearly inherent in the situation itself.
The overt efforts of the extreme left to influence the course of
public policy through violence and industrial strikes with the aim
of seizing power called forth a perfectly legitimate assertion of
governmental authority for the maintenance of law and order without

unduly violating constitutional freedoms. It would be naive to suppose that these liberties were designed to protect unconstitutional activities. The methods of the right, on the other hand, so skillfully concealed their real aim to overthrow the existing order that constitutional protection could be claimed successfully. For example, it was not apparent from the outset that the defamatory campaigns, directed against individuals and not against the "system," were an organized prelude to violence which required perhaps more serious attention than the more direct attacks of the left.

Although the government's right to proceed with every available means against the illegitimate use of force is undeniable, the severity of restrictive measures against the leftist press frequently did not seem warranted by the actual extent of the emergency. It appears doubtful for example that the strikes precipitated by the disagreements over the law concerning workers' councils were sufficiently grave to justify the prohibition of newspapers. Surely the public order could have been protected by holding the press to its social responsibility and by bringing offenders to justice in courts of law through prompt trials. But even if one were to grant the inevitability of the most drastic measures against the press, there was little justification for the virtually complete surrender of the civil administration to military authorities. During the controversy over the workers'-council law, prohibitions of publications were issued in some parts of the <u>Reich</u> by military commanders. This transfer of authority constituted a particularly severe threat to the leftist press in view of the well-known hostility of the majority of officers against Socialists and republicans. However, the freedom of the press was also seriously endangered in areas which were not placed under military command by the lack of three essential safeguards: (1) suppression, even where necessary, should always have been accompanied by a specific statement of the reasons for such action; (2) the period of prohibition should have been limited; (3) the possibility of appealing to the courts, as provided for in the Press Law, should have been preserved. These defects were to a large measure the result of the laxity with which functions and means of action of the various branches of the government were differentiated. It appears that the government in decreeing emergency measures never had a very clear conception as to whether they were protective or punitive. There is little justification for the executive branch, even in emergency situations, to invade the province of the courts by inflicting punishment. It can act legitimately only in the interest of security. Obviously, administrative action for the latter purpose is subject to easy abuse, and this danger tends to increase with a defective separation of powers.

The Kapp Putsch

In March, 1920, the counterrevolutionary forces launched their first open attack on the republic. The power of the military had grown persistently ever since the young republic had relied upon its support against the extreme left. When the government decided in March, 1920, to dissolve two of the Free Corps, Marine Brigades Ehrhardt and Loewenfeld, which had figured prominently in the suppression of leftist uprisings, a concrete provocation to resist finally was given. Now the mistake of the Social Democrats in relying indiscriminately, in their struggle against the extreme left, upon imperial army officers of notorious antirepublican bias began to bear bitter fruit. It was evident that the army could be depended on if employed against the left, but that it could not be used against the right.[29] Therefore, the government was forced to withdraw in face of the advance on Berlin of the rather unimpressive forces of the Ehrhardt Brigade and leave control of the government to the new chancellor, Wolfgang Kapp. The appeal of the Social Democratic government to the laboring masses to resist the Kapp government by means of a general strike is a measure of its desperation and impotence in view of its earlier efforts to quell industrial strikes with the aid of the very forces which were attacking it now. However, since the army could not be depended upon for the support of the legitimate government, a general strike provided the only hope. The appeal to labor fell on fertile ground, and the Kapp cabinet was forced to resign within five days after its seizure of power.

After the failure of the Kapp Putsch the right reverted to its strategy of defamation. However, the tenor of the more conservative papers of the right was now less militant than it had been before. Moreover, the primary target of the Nationalist attack was shifted. Direct assaults on the government gave way to veiled attacks focused on the former enemy powers, the occupation of the Ruhr, Saar, and Schleswig, as well as the "black shame" (schwarze Schmach) referring to the employment of colored troops in the occupation of some parts of Germany. The implication that the republic was responsible for these strongly resented conditions was unmistakable. In fact, it was quite openly maintained that, had the republican government shown more strength, the conditions of the Treaty of Versailles would have been less disastrous.[30] The extreme right, however, persisted in its old defamatory tactics. Erich Ludendorff declared in an interview that under the present government Germany was bound to perish.[31] A Nationalist deputy in the Reichstag demanded that the nation be cleansed of corruption which had increased, as shown by the Erzberger case, through parliamentarism, gangsterism, and other excesses that had been prevalent ever since the revolution.[32] Many similar utterances could be cited. A recurrent motif were small items about Erzberger, who had become the primary whipping boy of the Nationalist press.

All such accusations, contrived for the systematic disparagement of the republic, were given prominent space in the rightist
press. Most of them were sufficiently vague and intangible to be
beyond the reach of the courts. Yet, they were exceedingly effective in undermining the confidence in the republic of ever widening
circles of the population. Although such attacks aggravated, or
perhaps even precipitated, political emergencies, no effective
action was taken. Constitutional emergency powers might have
been used profitably to forestall crises without necessarily discrediting the constitutional system. Judicial remedies were only
occasionally resorted to and with considerable timidity. One of
the more prominent cases of this nature was a suit brought against
the Kreuzzeitung which had stated in an article that "a government,
a press, a party, that tolerates the presence of traitors or gang-
sters within its ranks is not entitled to loyal criticism. Involun-
tarily one reaches for the clothes brush to clean one's sleeve in
case of an accidental contact with such people." The verdict
required no more than the destruction of the article in question
and of the lineotypes. [33] In view of the general political instability the action can hardly be regarded as excessive. Nor would
the accusation that criticism of the government was being silenced
merit serious attention. On the contrary, the wisdom of resorting
to judicial means may be questioned because of its inevitable ineffectiveness. The trivial nature of these cases did not warrant
judicial sanctions severe enough to act as a deterrent. Yet, any
lenient sentence would of necessity act as an encouragement to
actual and would-be offenders. It virtually assured them that the
courts were either powerless or unwilling to counter antirepublican activities of this type with severe sentences.

Red Armies

The Kapp Putsch, which had demonstrated beyond the shadow
of a doubt the extreme vulnerability of the republican government,
did not produce, as might have been expected, solidarity of the
various leftist parties. On the contrary, the extreme left regarded
the moment propitious to impress the government with its strength
and obtain the long-desired changes toward the full-fledged Socialist
system. It was easy enough to prolong the general strike for which
the government had pleaded only recently. Thus in Central Germany
and in the Ruhr area, laborers, who had combined into formidable
red fighting units in defense against the Putschists and their sym-
pathizers, defied the republican government and could easily be
used for violent action against it. [34] For its defense, the government could rely on the regular military machine reinforced by

volunteers, which, though of dubious loyalty in case of conflict with Nationalists, could be effectively employed against the left.

The government for political reasons obviously could not tolerate such powerful rival forces as the red armies backing up the regional general strikes. Moreover, a prolonged period of industrial inactivity in the most important industrial areas would have spelled economic disaster. The government therefore had no choice but to take drastic action against its opponents on the left. Once again it had to make an about-face and resort to emergency decrees under the authority of Article 48 pointing leftward. It appeared that emergency government was fast becoming the rule rather than the exception. In emulation of the state of war of the imperial constitution, civil administration was transferred to a military governor, who normally was the commander of the local military district. The aim was twofold: to enable the government to deal effectively with the disturbances, unimpeded by constitutional restraints, and to introduce temporarily a higher degree of centralization into a federally organized government to prevent the radicals of the left from gaining a foothold in some parts of the Reich which might serve them as a basis of operations for the seizure of power. These aims could not be attained as long as civil liberties remained in full force; therefore their suspension was the actual core of emergency measures. [35]

Among the civil liberties suspended, those of Article 118 occupied a prominent position, since it was their abuse that had given the primary impetus to the Communist insurrection of 1920. It would be difficult to perceive any rationality in the uprising had it not been for the persistent agitation carried on through Communist newspapers and assemblies. The inferior striking power of the Communists as compared with that of the regular military establishment would certainly have neutralized all Communist efforts unless the masses of the workers could be persuaded to resort to violence against the government. [36] The control of the means of mass communication was therefore of paramount importance. The emergency decrees, [37] which in some areas remained in effect for the greater part of the year, permitted any and all limitations upon the press irrespective of existing legislation. Since all executive authority was transferred to the minister of the army, the latter could afford the press some measure of protection by appointing a civilian commissioner whose consent, once the appointment had been made, was required for any curtailment of press activity. The inadequacy of this presumably protective device is apparent. First, the appointment of the commissioner was not mandatory. Second, the appointee was not likely to protect the press against the authority to which he owed his appointment. The press of the left could derive little comfort from the fact that the minister of the army, Gustav Noske, was a Socialist, since the government was completely dependent on the

good will of the higher army leadership and virtually its prisoner.
Severe penalties were provided for violations of the decrees of
military commanders. Measures against the press could be appealed
to an especially established committee of the Reichsrat. The conservative frame of mind characteristic of members of that body raises
doubts concerning the protection of the rights of the Communist press.
Yet, the fact that a special machinery for appeals was set up was an
encouraging sign, since it indicated an awareness of the peculiar vulnerability of the press to emergency measures.

The Era of Assassinations

Meanwhile the Nationalists relentlessly continued their campaign
against the new regime which they considered a mere "interregnum."
Yet, the government observed a peculiar indifference toward rightist
hostilities. It either did not realize the seriousness of these attacks
which were systematically building up a strong popular resentment or
felt incapable of dealing with them. The only defense seems to have
consisted in libel suits brought by the injured individuals. [38] These
suits actually proved harmful to the republican cause. Since truth
was a defense under German law, the slanderers were given a forum
for additional propaganda. If they could not substantiate their charges,
they normally were subjected to a light fine. Frequently, the courts
sympathetic to the defendants would be satisfied with the dubious
evidence they produced and merely fine them for the libelous language
they had used. [39]

Erzberger
The systematic campaign against the republic and its
leaders produced results. In the summer of 1921 the leader of the
Independent Socialist party in the Bavarian parliament, Karl Gareis,
was assassinated. On August 26, 1921, Erzberger became the
victim of an attack by two officers of the Ehrhardt Brigade, who
had participated in the Kapp Putsch. After the first unsuccessful
attempt on his life, which has been mentioned, the press of the
extreme right had glorified the young would-be assassin, and some
papers even declared quite openly their disappointment that the
attempt had miscarried. [40] But the enterprise, which had been
unsuccessful at its first try, was not abandoned, and Erzberger
had remained the number one whipping boy. For all the international
setbacks which the intransigence of the Allied powers inflicted upon
the German republic the right pointed an accusing finger at Erzberger
as the one primarily responsible. It was he who was believed to have
been the spiritus rector of the government and the chancellor. The
bullets which killed Erzberger were not directed so much against
him as against the republic. They were intended to intimidate its

leaders.[41] The reaction of the extreme Nationalist press was similar
to that following the first attempt on Erzberger's life. With much
foresight the moderately leftist Berliner Tageblatt demanded that
steps as uncompromising as those taken against the Communists now
be taken against the Nationalists; the republic would destroy itself if
it did not carry through its struggle for self-preservation with the
greatest. determination.[42]

It was at this point that the government began to recognize the
Nationalist scheme of undermining the republic by systematically
inciting public opinion against its leaders. The need for drastic
steps against the right appeared overwhelming and admitted of no
delay. Evidence is the proclamation of the emergency decree of
August 30, 1921,[43] which followed closely Erzberger's assassination.
That the novelty of this type of subversion had to be fought with other
means than the open insurrection of the Communists was, of course,
obvious. A rightist organization openly challenging the authority of
the government by using or threatening force against it was not in
evidence. Violence was applied by individuals against individuals,
and the maintenance of order was a police, rather than a military,
problem. The existence of a larger and well-organized pattern
underlying the individual acts of violence was not then known. However, such knowledge, had it existed, would not have been likely to
impel against the right near-belligerent measures similar to those
which had been invoked the preceding year against the left, since
the open sympathy of the armed forces with the rightist counterrevolutionaries severely restricted the discretion of the government.
It was therefore preferable not to turn the civilian administration
over to military commanders, but rather to counter the novel methods
of rightist subversion with measures designed to curb the irresponsibility of the press. Newspapers could now be suppressed for a period
up to two weeks if they incited to a forcible change or abolition of the
constitutions of the Reich or the Länder, to acts of violence against
representatives of the republican-democratic form of government,
to disobedience of laws or decrees. The same sanction applied to
glorifications of such acts and derision of the constitution or institutions of the state in a manner apt to disturb the peace. In case of
repetition publications could be prohibited for a period of three
months. The authority to pronounce prohibitions was vested in the
minister of the interior. Nonjudicial confiscation was extended beyond the provisions of the Press Law so as to include violations of
the emergency decrees. Appeal against the rather severe sanctions
could again be made to a committee of the Reichsrat.

The measures were in principle favorably received by the pro-
republican press, which felt that constitutional rights of those bent
upon their destruction of necessity had to be limited.[44] The only
apprehensions expressed were based on the fear that the restrictions
might lead to a general suppression of all criticism of the government

and be applied with greater severity against the left than against the right. [45]

The journalistic attacks on Erzberger did not cease with his death; his assassination was enthusiastically acclaimed by the Nationalist press. As a result, nine newspapers identified with the extreme right had been suppressed by September 1;[46] by September 16 the number had risen to twenty-eight. Of these, six were lifted by the authorities responsible for them because of legal apprehensions concerning retroactive measures, and nine as a result of intervention by the minister of the interior. Twenty were lifted altogether prior to their stipulated expiration. [47] Confusion and erroneous application of the measures could not, of course, be entirely avoided. The Supreme Court itself in one instance flagrantly violated a basic principle of the Rechtsstaat by sanctioning retroactive measures against the Nationalist Deutsche Zeitung based on its general character rather than on a specific violation. [48] However, such instances were relatively rare. The general moderation with which the emergency measures were applied to the press was indicated by the co-operative attitude of the more conservative Nationalist press. For example, the Deutsche Allgemeine Zeitung and the National-Liberale Korrespondenz commended the impartiality of the measures. [49] As a matter of fact, it was soon to become apparent that the decrees were applied with equal severity against the left and the right. [50]

The effectiveness of the emergency decrees was impaired by the refusal of the Bavarian government to enforce the orders of the central government. The difficulty was partly due to the fact that a state of emergency had been in force in Bavaria ever since the demise of the soviet republic. To this local state of emergency directed against the left was added that proclaimed by the central government aimed primarily against the right. Under its constitutional obligations, the Bavarian government was required to execute the orders of the central authorities even if they conflicted with its own. Federal jealousy would not, however, permit this implied transfer of executive authority to the government of the Reich. Hence, the Bavarian government refused to execute the prohibition orders issued by the federal government against such ultranationalist papers as the Miesbacher Anzeiger and the Voelkische Beobachter. [51] In the same vein, the Bavarian government would not enforce an order of the central government suppressing the München-Augsburger Abendzeitung because of an article disparaging the president of the Reich. [52] Eventually, a compromise between Bavaria and the Reich was reached which made concessions to the former's federal sensitivities. At the same time, the Bavarian state of emergency was lifted, so that the orders of the Reich government could be effectively enforced. [53]

The committee of the Reichsrat created by the emergency

decree to rule on appeals of suppressed newspapers did much to improve the status of the press under these extraordinary conditions. Appeals concerned primarily retroactive measures of the government prohibiting the publication of newspapers on the basis of articles antedating the proclamation of the decree. The government, contending that on the basis of their past performance the publications involved could be expected to attempt the subversion of the existing order, generally failed to convince the Reichsrat committee. Retroactive prohibitions, whether of a penal or executive nature, were declared nonpermissible and therefore lifted. [54]

The emergency measures were severely attacked by various press associations. One passed a resolution rejecting all restrictions of the press. [55] Another objected to an economic interference by the administration without judicial decision and without the possibility of appeal to the ordinary courts of law. [56] Further objections questioned the necessity for such stringent measures to accomplish the ends for which the emergency decree had been issued. The objection was also raised that the criteria for suppressions had not been circumscribed with enough precision and that no uniformity prevailed in the country, since the application had been left to local police authorities. [57]

Even though the seriousness of the emergency cannot be denied, the practice of taking application and interpretation of the measures so completely out of the hands of the judiciary and entrusting them to administrative agencies is difficult to justify. As far as regulation of the extraordinary conditions through administrative decree is concerned, much can be said for it. The awkwardness of the legislative process, especially in countries where the multiparty system has bred a general reluctance to form coalitions, seems to commend swift executive action where drastic steps are imperative to stem the wave of political murders. However, the emergency created by the assassination of Erzberger was not so acute that the courts had to be bypassed. There is little cogency in the often-repeated rationalization that the measures adopted were preventive and administrative in nature, rather than punitive. The tenuous line between these two types of restriction is frequently difficult, if not impossible, to discern. In actual fact, the suppression of publications was tantamount to severe punishment and sometimes struck deeper than more conventional sanctions. Quite obviously the underlying purpose was to deter newspapers through trenchant sanctions from publishing prohibited matters. [58] Surely, the discouragement of acts discountenanced by the existing order is in the last analysis the proper object of any system of criminal law. Rather, the difficulty had its causes in a faulty scheme of the separation of powers and the absence of a tradition of judicial independence. Quite naturally, there was not much incentive for the republican forces to remedy these defects, since the courts were staffed predominantly by old-time conservatives, who were in full sympathy with the political views of the ultranationalists.[59] Any strengthening of judicial power was likely to impede governmental attempts to restrain the rightist press. There is, however, no evidence that considerations of this nature were responsible for the provisions of the executive decree. In spite of the undeniable procedural shortcomings of the decree, the substantive freedom of the press to criticize the government remained unimpaired. The absence of any serious accusations alleging violations of that freedom is a testimonial to the self-restraint exercised by the government.

After the emergency had elapsed, the systematic slander campaign of the Nationalist press against the republic and its representatives was resumed. Statements favorable to the republic were branded as unpatriotic and antinational.[60] At the same time, the number of political leaders earmarked as targets for Nationalist violence was mounting. Early in June, 1922, an unsuccessful attempt was made on the life of the former chancellor, and then mayor of Kassel, Philip Scheidemann. Scheidemann, like Erzberger, had been the object of much vilification and had been accused of exploiting his official position for his own personal enrichment.[61] The reaction of the extreme Nationalist press followed the same pattern as after the Erzberger assassination. The conservative press of the right reacted more responsibly in condemning the attack. Although no evidence existed, it was suspected at this time that the assassination of prominent political leaders was part of a organized plot against the republic, connected with one of the secret organizations created for that purpose.[62]

Rathenau

During the early period of the republic, Nationalist propaganda was directed with particular vehemence against those groups which had traditionally been excluded from participation in public affairs: the Jews and the Socialists.[63] The Nationalist fury was unleashed with particular vehemence against Walter Rathenau, a Jew and foreign minister in the Wirth cabinet. Rathenau, committed to an international policy of fulfillment of the obligations resulting from the Treaty of Versailles, had been one of the primary targets of Nationalist propaganda ever since his rise to political prominence. By birth a Jew and by conviction a democrat in domestic politics and a pacifist and internationalist in foreign policy, he seemed to symbolize everything that was hateful to the Nationalists, who were still unwilling to acknowledge the defeat of imperial Germany and were harboring thoughts of revenge. Attacks upon Rathenau, in prose as well as in verse, were circulated by word of mouth and in the counterrevolutionary press, and were supported by political attacks in the Reichstag. During the early 20's of June, Rathenau's "policy of fulfilment" of Germany's obligations under the Treaty of Versailles was the subject of an interpellation in the Reichstag.

The Nationalist members were quick to attack that policy in uncompromising terms without, however, being able to offer any feasible
alternatives. "Rathenau let himself be taken in by Germany's
enemies," was Dr. Reichert's contention, while Dr. Carl Helfferich,
one of the most prominent Nationalist representatives, maintained
that the continuation of the policy of fulfilment would inevitably mean
Germany's doom. [64] Only a few days later Rathenau became the
victim of Nationalist assassins while on his way to his office.

The sinister role played by the Nationalist press was far more
complex than appears at first sight. Its methodical defamation of
prospective victims seemed to have struck a responsive chord among
the German people, who, presumably chafing under the rule of un-
wanted politicians, apparently were now organizing for self-defense.
This interpretation was implied in the statement made by the Socialist president of the Reichstag, Paul Löbe, during the mourning
session held for Rathenau, when he attributed the crime to the glorification of previous assassinations and the muddying of the memories
of the victims. It was also expressed by Ernst von Salomon, one of
the participants in the plot against Rathenau. [65] The opinion thus
created had the dual effect of securing the acquiescence of the people
in Nationalist activism and of confronting a democratic government
with the dilemma of having to strike down a seemingly direct expression of the popular will. It tended to conceal the fact that the popular
basis of this activism, if it existed at all, was an extremely narrow
one and that the assassinations fitted into a larger pattern laid out
by a small organized minority of Nationalist activists. However,
the counterrevolutionary organization, which was soon to be exposed,
was recognized early by the leftist and moderate parties; and the
government took immediate and decisive action by issuing, within
two days of Rathenau's assassination, an emergency decree designed
to curb the activities believed responsible for the crisis. A statement of the chancellor points up the targets at which the decree was
aimed: the incessant defamations which had made the leaders of the
republic open prey and were designed first to eliminate the leaders
and then the republic proper. [66] The decree[67] was in its essentials
similar to that issued after the assassination of Erzberger. However, there was an unmistakable shift in emphasis since the counterrevolutionary pattern was now more clearly recognized. While the
earlier measure was to cope with disobedience to the law, the new
decree was primarily directed against such defamation and derision
of political leaders as were apt to produce violence, glorification of
violence against the republic or present or former members of its
government, as well as direct incitement to violence. [68]

Jurisdiction over violations of the decree was entrusted to a
Court of State for the Protection of the Republic to be established
at the Supreme Court and composed of seven members (three judicial and four nonjudicial) appointed by the president of the Reich.

Confiscation and suppression of newspapers followed in essence the
corresponding provisions of the Press Law with the exception that
the government had the right of immediate appeal against a court
decision lifting confiscation, and that such an appeal had a delaying
effect. The decree caused less insecurity than that of the previous
year in that it defined punishable offenses with more precision. A
higher degree of uniformity in the enforcement of the provisions was
attained through a transfer of jurisdiction from the local courts to a
central judicial body. On the negative side, the elaborate safeguards
of the Press Law of 1874, which had created procedurally a presump-
tion in favor of the press, were abandoned. Court decisions in favor
of the press could not be acted upon until a decision had been rendered
on the appeal of the government. The administration could prohibit
publications in the interest of public order without a previous confiscation order by the courts. The duration of a prohibition was wholly
subject to administrative determination within the four weeks' limit
provided for. Needless to say, the periods of prohibition, set by the
executive department without any external checks, were sufficiently
long to constitute a serious financial embarrassment to the papers
affected.

The emergency decree had been subjected to a critical discussion in the Reichstag the day before its promulgation.[69] The
recurrent theme sounded by the left was the fear that the measures,
though aimed at the political excesses of the extreme right, might
boomerang if applied by an administration or judiciary of a decidedly
rightist bias. It was even demanded that the decree be so formulated
as specifically to preclude its application to labor organizations.[70]
Such a specification would have expressed the spirit of the decree.
In fact, the intention to curb rightist radicalism was explicitly confirmed by the Socialist minister of justice, Gustav Radbruch.[71] The
chancellor himself, in a dramatic speech in the Reichstag, had pointed
an accusing finger at the parties of the extreme right when he exclaimed:
"Der Feind steht rechts!" The same note was struck by moderate and
rightist political parties. Centrist representative Wilhelm Marx conceded that the decrees were directed primarily against the right,
since it had forced the government to resort to extraordinary measures
in self-defense.[72] Even on the right the justification of emergency
action was not denied, since some groups, in resorting to extraconstitutional means, had placed themselves outside the pale of constitutional
guarantees. Their only explicit apprehensions were related to the
fear that certain groups of citizens might be victimized because of
their political views.[73] This seemingly conciliatory and constructive
attitude was perhaps less the result of fair-minded objectivity than
an early indication of the long-range strategy to be employed by the
radicals of the right for the subversion of the republic under the cover
of constitutional guarantees. As long as the plan did not include the
violent overthrow of the republic but contemplated a more subtle

form of subversion, they could easily benefit from constitutional liberties which tied the hands of the government but not of the opposition. On the moderate right, the People's party was generally in favor of the emergency measures but insisted on their impartial application to left and right alike. [74]

The Court of State, which was to be set up to adjudicate cases arising under the emergency decree, came in for severe criticism from all quarters. The left objected to the appointment of professional judges as part of the personnel of the court. It was felt that since a two-thirds majority was required for a conviction, the lay judges would be impotent unless they could enlist the support of at least one of the professional judges. The expectation that many judges who were loyal to the republic could be found was slight. [75] The right, on the other hand, objected to the participation of lay judges which would degrade the court to a political tribunal. The four lay judges, they feared, would be strictly political appointments. [76] A further major objection of the left had reference to the execution of the measures decreed by the Reich government by local authorities. The Bavarian precedent made it appear likely that the intent of the central government would be frustrated or rendered ineffective by rightist Länder governments. [77]

An objective evaluation of the situation clearly demonstrates the need for extraordinary measures. Attempted and actual assassinations had occurred with increased frequency. It had also come to light that one of the secret organizations, Organisation Consul, had formed a blast-and-murder detachment to perform assassinations of political leaders and other terrorist acts. The membership of the assassins of Rathenau in that detachment was established. Their plan to assassinate twelve leading personalities, including the banker Max Warburg and the editor of the Berliner Tageblatt, Theodor Wolff, had been revealed. [78] The new restrictions of the press, issued in the knowledge of this acute danger, varied in essence from those of the previous year in only two respects: the possible duration of prohibitions was extended and the prison sentence, which had been optional before, was now mandatory. The fact that the plans of the secret murder organization had finally been revealed lent considerable merit to the continued practice of leaving the issuance of prohibition orders to administrative initiative. The emergency decree as such was in no way discriminatory. More problematical was the impartiality of the personnel of administrative and judicial agencies whose discretion was extensive. However, the decrees are perhaps most vulnerable from the point of view of their efficacy. Since they were emergency, that is, extraordinary and temporary, measures provoked by a threat to the existing order, they might have served their purpose more effectively had they been explicitly directed against the quarters that were responsible for the crisis. It is perhaps one of the weaknesses of constitutional democracies that they can only with difficulty proceed against their foes in time

of emergency without simultaneously inflicting harm on potentially
friendly forces. Even so, the extraordinary impartiality of the
decree of 1922 reveals a fundamental misconception of the nature
and ends of emergency action. Since its primary purpose is the
temporary suspension of normal constitutional restraints to counter
an acute threat to the established order, it would have been quite
proper to direct the measure specifically against the quarters from
which the challenge emanated. The moment was probably opportune
for dealing a decisive blow to the radicals of the right. They had
committed open acts of violence, and their subversive plans had
become manifest. Such a course of action might have promised
success since the left was united for the first time in its determination to protect the republic against the counterrevolutionary
forces. [79] The opportunity was missed, partly because of the neutral
formulation of the decree, and partly because of the perversion of
its purposes by the judiciary. [80]

The neutral formulation of the emergency measures permitted
considerable variety in their application, since much of the detail
of their execution was left to the governments of the Länder. Consequently, in Prussia, where a government dominated by Social
Democrats was in office, the decree was largely applied against
the right. [81] In Bavaria, on the other hand, the left was the main
target. Several Communist newspapers were suppressed on the
basis of articles critical of the negative attitude of the prime
minister toward the measures taken or contemplated by the government of the Reich for the protection of the republic. [82] The legitimacy of such action was based on Article 48 of the constitution,
which vested emergency powers in the governments of the Länder
to deal with local emergencies. The Bavarian government was
therefore able to suppress leftist criticism directed against the
enemies of the republic.

The Law for the Protection of the Republic

Soon after the issuance of the decree a conference of minister presidents decided that an early substitution of a legislative act for the decree would be desirable. [83] The Law for the Protection of the Republic was enacted by the Reichstag on July 21, 1922, to be effective for five years. [84] It seems rather strange at first sight that an emergency situation should be dealt with by a regular legislative act. The debates on the bill in the Reichstag reveal that there were more cogent reasons than merely a peculiar German emphasis on legalism. It was a matter of general knowledge that the crisis had been the result of long-term preparations. It appeared doubtful therefore that the temporary and extraordinary remedy of executive decree would be adequate. [85] For three years a relentless campaign had been systematically carried on by the press against the leaders of the republic. Under the regular laws the incitement to violence against such personalities had been punished with only nominal fines. It was therefore intended to make more severe sentences mandatory for such offenses through a special law. [86] The experiences of the past no doubt seemed to justify long-range measures for the prevention and liquidation of emergencies. After an assassination had taken place, the rightist press normally conducted itself with moderation during the relatively short life span of the executive decree, so that the decrees soon lost their raison d'être. However, once they were repealed, the campaigns were resumed full blast. The moderate right favored the act because it might minimize the legal insecurity which had prevailed under the executive decrees. [87] The left, on the other hand, suspicious of the rightist bias of the judiciary, preferred administrative jurisdiction to that of the regular courts provided by the new law.

The law was essentially similar to the emergency decrees which had preceded it. The most notable difference was the more precise definition of the "republic" which it aimed to protect. The emergency decrees had professed to protect the "republican form of government." This, in theory, did not merely embrace the republic which had been established by the Weimar constitution, but any republican form of government, including soviet republics advocated by the Communist and Independent Socialist parties. While this formulation was temporarily useful, the long-range character of the legislative act, which was to become part of the general legal order, required a more precise terminology. Obviously, the republic could not stand by idly when its

overthrow in favor of a republic not resting on a parliamentary
basis was being engineered. The law had therefore to be formulated in such a way as to prohibit any change in the existing
constitutional order through extraconstitutional means. Hence
it defined as a punishable offense vilification or derision of the
republican form of government as determined by the constitution.
This qualification was adopted upon the insistence of the right
and over the objections of the left. [88] As far as the composition of the Court of State was concerned, concessions were made
to the left. Its membership was raised to nine, three of whom
were to be members of the Supreme Court while the remaining
six did not have to qualify for judicial office. Thus the trained
judges could be outvoted by the lay judges. The admittedly political nature of the lay judges greatly perturbed the Nationalist
party. [89] The basis for their fears lay in the political one-sided-
ness of the previous Court of State which had been established
under the emergency decree. Its lay members had been almost
exclusively identified with the Centrist, Democratic, and the two
Socialist parties. The Nationalists were not alone in expressing
these apprehensions. Even the moderate republican forces re-
quested a complete depoliticization. [90] This claim was of course
incapable of realization. Since a nonpolitical judiciary did not
exist in Germany at the time, the leftist coloration of the lay
judges was amply counterbalanced by the antirepublican bias of
the professional judges. [91] Yet, the government committed itself to a reduction of the percentage of parliamentarians among
the lay judges. [92]

The provisions specifically affecting the press did not de-
viate to any significant extent from those of the emergency decree. On the procedural side, an attempt was made to reduce
the possibilities of friction between Reich and Länder in their
execution. The Reich minister of the interior was given authority to request specific state action, and federal conflicts were to
be settled definitively by the Court of State. Thereby a federal
compromise was provided for ensuring, in theory, the priority
of the Reich over the Länder. In practice, however, Bavaria
entered upon a path of open revolt against the jurisdiction of the
Reich.

The Law for the Protection of the Republic had hardly
been proclaimed when the Bavarian government issued a decree
of its own under the authority of Article 48 of the Weimar constitution[93] to substitute for the federal law in the part of Bavaria east of the river Rhine. Its provisions were in essence identical with those of the federal law except that it substituted for
the jurisdiction of the federal agencies that of the Land. The
Bavarian People's Courts, ill-famed because of their open hostility against the left, [94] were given jurisdiction over matters

arising under the Protection Law. The control of the Reich
minister of the interior over prohibition of assemblies and publications was repudiated. The reasons for the countermeasure
were clearly stated: (1) the political composition of the Court
of State was considered a violation of the constitution as well as
of democratic principles in general; (2) the adoption of the Law
over the objections of the Bavarian government allegedly had
aroused in Bavaria an extraordinary resentment, which would
endanger public safety if the Law were enforced without qualification. The unconstitutionality of the Bavarian measure admits of no doubt.[95] Hence, the government of the Reich had two
alternative courses of action: (1) it could take the matter to the
Supreme Court as a federal conflict; or (2) it could enforce the
law of the Reich by sending troops to Bavaria under the authority
of Article 48 (Reichsexekutive). The government did neither,
but attempted a settlement through negotiations with the Bavarian government.[96] A compromise was reached whereby, in
return for substantial concessions by the Reich, Bavaria agreed
to repeal its decree.[97] The central government conceded that
only matters of utmost gravity would be referred to the Court of
State. The chief prosecutor of the Reich, in conducting police
activities in Bavaria, would avail himself of state police forces.
The members of the Court of State would not be selected from a
political point of view but on the basis of their personal qualifications. Their selection would also take into account the special
interest of the various Länder. Therefore a second senate for
South Germany would be formed at the Court of State in consultation with the respective state governments to which cases involving South German affairs would be referred.[98] Quite obviously a regional arrangement such as this constituted a substantive
impairment of the central authority. Only in the most formal
sense was its jurisdiction preserved.

    The enactment of the Law marked the disintegration of the
solidary front which, after the assassination of Rathenau, had
extended from the extreme left to the center. The left objected
to the Law because of its leniency and because of the tendency to
leave prosecution and enforcement in the hands of the regular
agencies, whose personnel was of such caliber as to render an
effective enforcement unlikely. If times were such as to warrant
extraordinary measures, their enforcement, it was felt, might
well have been left to special agencies.[99] The Communists were
apprehensive out of fear that the effect of the Law would be the
silencing of all opposition regardless of whether it emanated from
the left or the right.[100]

    Numerous suppressions of newspapers and periodicals in
all parts of the Reich followed the enactment of the Protection
Law. In perusing the moderate press of the period one gains the

impression that the law was certainly not applied with greater
severity against the right than against the left. The fact that the
suppressions of the rightist press were not unwarranted seems
indicated by the repeated suppression of the ultranationalist
Voelkischer Beobachter and Miesbacher Anzeiger by the rightist
Bavarian government. That there were occasional transgressions
of administrative authority is only natural in the absence of prior
judicial confirmation. The repeated repeals of prohibition orders
by the Court of State indicate that quite clearly. [101] The temptation to utilize suppression to dispose of criticism was at times
too great for local authorities to resist. Nonetheless it has to
be admitted that the government made an honest attempt to be
fair in applying the Law against offenders of the left and of the
right. For example, both the Nationalist Berliner Lokal-Anzeiger
and the Communist Rote Fahne were prohibited for equal periods,
and in both cases the Prussian minister of the interior was willing
to revoke the prohibition against an undertaking to discontinue
defamation of the republic. [102]

The problem of how to deal with occasional violations by
the friendly, or at least not aggressively hostile, press posed a
special dilemma for the government. A case in point was the
suppression for eight days of the moderately rightist Deutsche
Allgemeine Zeitung owned by the industrialist Hugo Stinnes. The
prohibition was occasioned by the assertion that the "so-called"
German government, due to its "proverbial unreliability," had
lost all respect and credit abroad. [103] Although the law was
formally applicable in this instance, the moderate Frankfurter
Zeitung questioned the wisdom of the steps taken because of this
rather innocuous criticism. [104] Moreover, the Deutsche Allgemeine Zeitung had only a limited distribution and was read almost exclusively by upper-middle-class groups not easily given
to rash emotional outbursts. A paper of this type was hardly in
a position to endanger the security of the republic. The prohibition, as the Frankfurter Zeitung pointed out, gave the Deutsche
Allgemeine Zeitung a significance which it had not had before,
and was apt to create the impression that the purpose of the Protection Law was to stifle all criticism and eliminate the freedom of the press altogether. [105] This view, which at first sight
might appear as a repudiation of the principle of equality before
the law, was actually quite sensible in the light of the peculiar
circumstances surrounding the genesis of the Protection Law.
The law was not conceived as a permanent standard for individual liberties, but rather as a measure of expediency to deal with
a special and, it was hoped, temporary situation. Since its
basic purpose was the preservation of the constitutional order in
face of internal danger, it aimed at the consequences of an act
rather than at the moral and legal justification of the act itself.

It is in this light that the application of the Law has to be viewed.
In fact, its opportunistic character was manifest from the optional nature of its sanctions. The discretion which was thereby left
to judicial and administrative agencies was certainly not exercised with discernment in the case of the Deutsche Allgemeine
Zeitung. Its prohibition, which was not necessitated by considerations of security, was clearly a violation of the freedom of
the press. By no stretch of the imagination could it stand the
clear-and-present-danger test. The Protection Law itself could
no doubt be justified in terms of that standard, since in making
the sanctions optional, the legislators left discretion to administrative and judicial agencies to determine in individual cases
the requirements of public safety. It was therefore up to these
agencies to subject each suppression to a rigorous scrutiny in
terms of the clear-and-present-danger test. In applying this extreme sanction to the Deutsche Allgemeine Zeitung, the government not only ignored that standard but also demonstrated its
misconception of the fundamental purpose of the Law to deal with
the tactics employed by totalitarian parties which relied on emotional appeals to the uneducated masses rather than to educated
groups.

It would be illuminating to examine the practice of the
Court of State in relation to the press under the measures adopted
for the protection of the republic. Unhappily, the complete decisions were never published, and one has to rely on the few excerpts published occasionally in legal journals. A further aid is
a compilation by the Reich ministry of the interior of the decisions of the Court of State covering, however, only the earliest
period of its activities. [106] Obviously the cases reported in excerpts do not tell the whole story. With only few exceptions the
sentences imposed by the Court are not mentioned. This information is actually indispensable for an accurate evaluation of the
Court's activities, since any possible bias cannot be deduced
from convictions and acquittals alone. Far more revealing would
be a comparative study of the harshness or leniency of the punish-
ments meted out to the left and right, respectively. Nor do the
published excerpts disclose the complete factual background, or
give in all cases the full name of the newspapers or dates of publication of offensive articles; nor do they indicate the political
affiliation of the publication involved, though this frequently is
apparent from the tenor of the decision. It is, therefore, often
impossible to refer back to the original publication in order to establish more fully the circumstances which had provoked repressive measures. Hence a comprehensive picture of the application
of the Protection Law cannot be unfolded. However, on the basis
of the available information general trends are discernible concerning the questions which are of primary interest in the context

of this study: (1) whether the Law was utilized to stifle criticism
of the government generally; and (2) whether the decisions of the
Court reveal any bias in favor of either the left or the right.

As far as the first question is concerned, the Court made
it clear that it was not its function to suppress criticism of the
government; rather, its province was to determine from case to
case where the line was to be drawn between a sharp, though legitimate, criticism and a vilification of the government by the
press. [107] In performing this task, the Court did not normally
take a bigoted stand. It declared repeatedly that the expression
of monarchical ideas and a refutation of the republican form of
government were insufficient reasons for the suppression of publications. [108] However, in matters involving defamation of assassinated members of the government, the Court objected, for
example, to the assertion that Rathenau's Jewish affiliations
caused him to act in a manner designed to humiliate Germany. [109]
On the other hand, the Court did not take issue with an article
stating that the termination of Rathenau's activities was no misfortune and that the Jew Rathenau was a parasite, since this in its
view merely represented the matter-of-fact expression of an opinion in an objective situation. [110] The following passage from an
article was considered unobjectionable by the Court: ''When formerly a Jewish communist shot down a Christian minister, the
entire Jew press acclaimed and called the cowardly assassinator
a hero; but when now Christian fanatics shoot down a Jew all of
Judah is wailing furiously and curses not only the murderer...,
but one curses millions of people who did not know the murderer
and who could not restrain him but who are suspected of not
joining in the hysterical clamor of the Jewish press.''[111] On the
other hand, the Court objected to a reference to the government
as the Berlin branch of the Muscovite Soviet government;[112] to a
description of Germany's condition as the glorious era of tyranny;[113]
to a reference to Chancellor Joseph Wirth as the responsible leader of German policy under which the Jews enjoy more rights than
Germans;[114] to the charge that the Protection Law was not passed
for the purpose of protecting the constitution but rather for the protection of the Jews;[115] to the accusation that influential personalities had used the assassination of Rathenau for the consolidation
of their own shaky positions; and to the description of Rathenau as
a representative of international Jewish high finance who had
abused his high office for his own benefit and to the detriment of
Germany. [116]

On the other hand, the Court was tolerant of a severe criticism of the policy of fulfillment, which it considered a legitimate
function of the press, [117] and of the charge that the government
favored a campaign of hatred among the political parties and that
it had systematically stimulated an increasing tension. [118]

These random samples may suffice to convey an idea of the scope of freedom permitted the press under the Law for the Protection of the Republic. They do not admit of the conclusion that the Court acquiesced in its use for the sole purpose of stifling criticism embarrassing to the government. By and large, prohibitions were upheld only when the objectionable publication was devoid of a factual basis and apt to endanger the constitutional order under the then prevailing tense conditions. Surely, all severe but justified criticism could without question have been expressed just as effectively in a more restrained form. As far as genuine criticisms were concerned, the Court certainly went far to condone them, even if the manner of presentation was not strictly in keeping with the requirements of the Law. In fact, if the Court is subject to criticism, it should be leveled at its frequent leniency, rather than stringency, toward rightist defamations. It generally tended to draw the lines between permissible sharp satire and vilification in favor of the defendant, even in cases where restrictions would have been legitimate by any standard. For example, anti-Semitic outbursts, apt further to arouse the already tense emotions to the point of total disruption of social harmony, were condoned by the Court, although under the then prevailing conditions they warranted an invocation of the sanctions of the Protection Law. The decisions of the Court against publications disparaging the flag of the republic may appear pedantic to the observer. Yet, it would have been folly to ignore the actual seriousness of such attacks in view of the importance attached by a strongly nationalistic people to national symbols. Their effects were further aggravated by the widespread resentment against the abolition of the black-white-red colors of imperial Germany. To many Germans the new colors were nothing but symbols of defeat and national disgrace.

The scanty information available precludes an accurate appraisal of the severity of the Court's actions toward offenders of the left and of the right respectively. However, newspaper notices regarding the repeal of prohibition orders by the Court of State against Communist newspapers hardly leave room for any intimation that the practices of the Court were highly discriminatory.[119]

The frequently voiced criticism that the Law for the Protection of the Republic was designed to silence the opposition[120] thus had little basis in fact. Unless anarchy was to prevail, expression dedicated to perverted ends had, of course, to be limited. When it leaves the arena of rational debate and unharnesses violent action, discussion is incompatible with social order and forfeits constitutional protection. There had been no prosecutions in the German republic because of antirepublican attitudes or the expression of antirepublican sentiments until conspiracy and overt

crimes seemed to undermine its very foundation. [121] Even the
Protection Law as an extraordinary measure was not directed
only against some political movements but applied impartially to
all violators regardless of their political coloration. It is quite
evident that the government attempted to depoliticize through this
enactment a situation which required decisive political action.
The primary overt reason for enacting a special law was the need
for more severe penalties and a more precise definition of illegal
activities. However, the most compelling reason was perhaps
the antirepublican bias of the judiciary, which necessitated a
transfer of enforcement to administrative or special judicial
agencies.

The Fechenbach Case

Another method of subverting the republic, pursued systematically only at a later time, was the instigation of a series of
treason trials ushered in by the famous Fechenbach case which
coincided with the trial of the accessories to the Rathenau assassination. [122] Felix Fechenbach, member of the Independent Social Democratic party and former secretary to the Bavarian prime
minister, Kurt Eisner, was indicted before the People's Court in
Munich for having turned over to the Swiss journalist Payot, in
April of 1919, diplomatic documents which were published in the
Parisian newspaper Le Journal in support of the then progressing
anti-German campaign. As a consequence, the indictment stated,
the peace terms of the Treaty of Versailles were harsher than they
might otherwise have been. The court held that Fechenbach had
intended to advance the victory of bolshevism by intensifying the
intransigence of the Allies toward Germany and sentenced him for
treason to ten years in a penitentiary. The conviction disregarded
the fact that the documents in question had merely historical significance, that they had already been released in part, and that the
governments of the Reich and Bavaria had announced the imminent
release of the remainder. It also was proved that the information
in question had had no bearing whatever on the peace terms. [123]
The historical expert who had testified in the trial publicly labeled
the decision a miscarriage of justice because of the insignificance
of the Fechenbach information for Germany's international position. [124] A second charge preferred against Fechenbach involved
the release to a Berlin news agency of information concerning
events within antirepublican and illegal secret organizations, questions of the Bavarian home guard, Communist agitation, discussion
of Russian monarchists, and separatist tendencies in Bavaria.
This information was eventually passed on to Dutch and British
newspapers. Against the contention that the duty of the accused to

treat some of the items transmitted as secret was "self-evident,"
Fechenbach maintained that he had considered it his duty to disclose information on antirepublican secret organizations which
endangered the republic as well as international peace. He felt
that the public discussion of such organizations in Germany and
abroad was indispensable to fight the counterrevolution in Bavaria.
The court held that Fechenbach had committed a criminal offense,
since the publication of this information contained at least an implicit accusation of the toleration by German authorities of secret
munitions depots in violation of Germany's obligations under the
Treaty of Versailles. Fechenbach was sentenced for "attempted
treason" to five years' imprisonment, although it could not be
proved that the information had actually been published. The implications of this decision for the freedom of the press were
serious indeed. True reports disclosing the existence of organizations that were illegal under municipal and international law
would from now on be punishable as treason. It does not require
much ingenuity to recognize the court's attempt to intimidate supporters of the republic in order to prevent any future public disclosures embarrassing to the enemies of the republic.

The Fechenbach decision created widespread consternation.
The press considered it a fundamental attack on its freedom. Ap-
prehension was expressed not only by the press of the left and
center, but even by such Nationalist papers as the Berliner Lokal-
Anzeiger[125] and Der Tag.[126] Equally, the Association for the
Protection of German Authors objected that the principles applied
in the Fechenbach case constituted a threat to the freedom of
writing guaranteed in the constitution.[127] The Association of Republican Judges protested against the conviction, the procedures
used, and the extent of the punishment.[128]

The widespread campaign for the restoration of justice
waged by the press of varied political complexions soon produced
effects. The Fechenbach decision was debated in the Reichstag
in July, 1923, and by this time the Bavarian government was sufficiently embarrassed to declare its willingness to parole Fechenbach. The sentence was substantially reduced, and after serving
for two years and four months Fechenbach was released. The
moral courage demonstrated by the French courts in setting aright
a grievous wrong by clearing Alfred Dreyfus of his guilt in the
early part of the century was clearly lacking in the action taken to
repair the damage of the Fechenbach case. Fechenbach was not
cleared but merely paroled. However, the embarrassment to the
Bavarian government was only imperfectly concealed, and the
implicit admission of impropriety through the release of Fechenbach was generally apparent. In fact, his release was considered
everywhere as tantamount to an admission of his innocence.[129]

Inflation and Strikes

The first half of the year 1923 was a period of relative political calm which, however, was deceptive and only of short
duration. The decision of the federal government to counter the
French invasion of the Ruhr area with passive resistance produced a solidarity of most political parties which was reminis-
cent of the national-unity front of August, 1914. [130] However,
even then there were forewarnings of the political outbursts
which in the latter part of the year were to test to the full the
ability of the government to pilot the ship of state through the
dangers emanating from both the extreme right and the extreme
left. The presence on German soil of a foreign invader who
could be fought only with such nonbelligerent means as passive
resistance was too good an opportunity to be missed by the extreme right, which was then consolidating its strength in Bavaria. Significantly, demonstrations staged in Munich by the young
National-Socialist party were directed, not against the French
invader, but rather against the "November criminals." The
movements of the extreme right could easily take root in Bavaria, where a rightist government afforded them benevolent treatment. The National-Socialist party enjoyed extensive immunities
in spite of frequent violations of the Protection Law and persistent public disturbances. By contrast, the Prussian government
recognized the serious danger emanating from the right and proceeded decisively against the northern counterpart of the
National-Socialist party, the Racist Freedom party (Deutsch-
Voelkische Freiheitspartei). At the same time, the Communists
increased their activities in Central Germany, precipitating considerable political unrest. The federal government reprimanded
the governments of Saxony and Thuringia while ignoring similar
subversive activities of the right in Bavaria. It is understand-
able that such discriminatory treatment was strongly resented by
the left. However, any condemnation of the indulgence of the
federal government toward rightist excesses in Bavaria over-
looks the fact that it did not dispose of forces which could be employed against the right. [131]

By the summer of 1923 strikes had become a frequent occurrence in various parts of the country due to the bottomless
inflation. In some instances they developed into full-fledged rebellions. Under these circumstances the government once again
had to resort to emergency powers to curb journalistic excesses. [132] Punishable offenses were circumscribed somewhat
more broadly then in the Protection Law. Publications could

now be suppressed because of incitement to overthrow forcibly
the constitutionally determined republican form of government
or because of an appeal to violence in a manner endangering the
public peace. The vague and more inclusive phrasing of the decree could easily make it a catchall for a wide range of offenses.
On the procedural side, jurisdiction was transferred from state
to federal authorities. The possibility of appeal by state and
municipal authorities to the Court of State was abolished. Thus,
at least in theory, the federal difficulties of dealing with obsti-
nate states such as Bavaria, Saxony, and Thuringia were finally
removed. However, in actual practice this end was not achieved,
since local police authorities retained the power to confiscate
newspapers and prohibit their publication in case of clear and
present danger (bei Gefahr im Verzuge). The vagueness and
flexibility of that clause virtually precluded any possibility of federal protection of the press against interference by state authorities.

The government justified the issuance of the decree in terms
of the extraconstitutional agitation of the Communist press. For
example, the Rote Fahne had admonished labor organizations to
join forces for the immediate establishment of a labor government, adding that a government of workers and peasants could not
be created through parliamentary means but only "through the
fight of the street against the parliamentary government."[133]
The Tribüne of Magdeburg had asserted that the dissolution of the
Reichstag should be forced through a nationwide general strike.[134]
In the light of these examples the necessity for extraordinary
measures can hardly be questioned. Even under their provisions,
the workers retained the right to strike for improved social and
economic conditions within the established governmental framework. However, the use of the economic weapon of the strike to
exert an influence on parliamentary processes through violence
was a different matter. Thus, the Communist objection to these
measures had little basis in fact. The more direct affectation of
the Communist than of the rightist press lay in the nature of the
matter. The rightist press minimized incitement to open and organized revolt against authority and relied on the more subtle
method of directing vague emotional appeals to the desperate people.

It might seem strange at first sight that the expressions
mentioned above should have impelled drastic emergency measures.
Yet, the extraordinary action appears less ludicrous in the light
of the then existing political-economic tensions. The continuously
mounting inflationary pressure was driving people to desperation
and causing strike waves of considerable magnitude which, in
turn, aggravated the already depressed economy. The French
occupation of the Ruhr had caused considerable Nationalist-Socialist

activity in Bavaria, which in turn provoked increased Communist unrest in Central Germany. At the Bavarian boundary ad-
joining Central Germany open warfare could be expected any
minute. General starvation was a real possibility. It is apparent that a people subjected to such tensions over a period of
several months could easily be aroused by inflammatory appeals
of the press. Irresponsible newspapers capitalizing on these
difficulties therefore had to be curbed.

Nationalist Rumblings in Bavaria

Under the pressure of the rapidly progressing inflation the
government was forced to call off the passive resistance against
the French occupation of the Ruhr. This national humiliation
provided an opportunity for Nationalist groups to intensify their
antirepublican activities, which had been stirring in Bavaria for
some time. In anticipation of disturbances, the Bavarian government invoked emergency powers under Article 48 of the federal constitution, suspending civil rights and transferring all
administrative powers to the monarchist, Gustav von Kahr, as
state commissioner. The tenor of the decree as well as the personality of the state commissioner were hardly designed to elicit
much rejoicing in Berlin. To forestall the possibility of sabotage
by the Bavarian government, the central government countered
with an emergency decree transferring the entire executive authority to the commanders of the various army districts. [135] Once
again the press was the primary target, since Section 1 provided:
"Article 118 of the federal constitution is suspended until further
notice. Consequently, limitations... of the freedom of the press
are permissible also beyond the designated legal limits." Thereby all remaining minimum guarantees of the press were temporarily abandoned and the press left to the mercy of the federal
minister of the army. This was in essence a return to the state
of war which could be invoked in imperial Germany in case of
emergency and transcended all previous encroachments committed by the republic. It was not until three months later that
the right of appeal to the Court of State against suppression of
newspapers under this decree was introduced. [136]
Although the decree was admittedly an outgrowth of the Nationalist excitement caused by the German defeat in the Ruhr
struggle and of the excesses of such Nationalist newspapers as
the Voelkische Beobachter, the Bavarian government once again
assumed a very indulgent attitude toward the radicals of the right
while proceeding with vigor against the left. The federal government was again powerless to enforce its measures against Bavaria, while it restrained successfully the Socialist-Communist

governments of Central Germany. [137] Within the first few days
of the state of emergency a considerable number of Communist
newspapers were suppressed. [138] The actual application of the
emergency measures again followed the pattern which by now had
become familiar: the initial impetus for the decree was the antirepublican activities of the extreme right in Bavaria, while in effect it was applied with vigor only against the left. This anti-
leftist bias was directed not only against the extraconstitutional
forces but also against papers identified with parties supporting
the constitution. A virtual press censorship was exercised by the
military. Thus the Democratic Berliner Volkszeitung was suppressed because it had printed information concerning the uprising
of the illegal defense organizations (schwarze Reichswehr) in
Küstrin under the leadership of Major Bruno Ernst Buchrucker,
although these events had already been reported in the foreign
press. [139]

Discrimination against the press of the left was nothing new
in Bavaria. Ever since the issuance of the Bavarian emergency
decree of May 11, 1923, which was occasionally referred to as
the "Bavarian Anti-Socialist Law,"[140] the Bavarian government
had proceeded vigorously against the Social Democratic and the
Communist press. With only few exceptions, the Social Democratic press was suppressed at one time or another, whereas
the utmost leniency was shown offenders of the extreme right. [141]
Paradoxical as it may seem, the grounds for suppressing Social
Democratic papers at times were disclosures of National-Socialist
mobilization for the forcible seizure of power. In other words,
the Bavarian emergency decree for all practical purposes was a
protective measure for the benefit of the enemies of the Weimar
constitution, the federal emergency decree of September 26 notwithstanding. A conflict between the federal government and
Bavaria was thus inevitable. Once again a crisis was precipitated
when the federal minister of war ordered the local military commander, General von Lossow, to prohibit publication of the Voelkische Beobachter. The impotence of the federal government was
only too clearly revealed when the Bavarian government refused
to carry out its order and von Lossow declared his primary allegiance to Bavaria. When after some delay the prohibition order
was finally executed, the Nationalist state government compen-
sated for its loss of face by simultaneously prohibiting the Democratic Nürnberger Morgenpresse. The latter was informed of its
suppression for two weeks by telephone, without subsequent
written confirmation and without indication of the grounds. There
was a widespread, and apparently not unfounded, suspicion in
circles sympathetic to the republican government that a causal
connection existed between the suspension of the two papers, and
that the prohibition of the loyal paper was a mere retaliation for

the suppression of an extreme rightist paper. [142] The eventual
formal compliance with the federal order was not, of course,
tantamount to effective enforcement. The day after the prohibition had been proclaimed the Voelkische Beobachter was still
sold openly in some parts of the state by uniformed National-
Socialists in full purview of the police. [143] Later the same month,
when the crisis gained momentum, Bavaria entered upon a path
of open revolt against the federal government in requiring federal
troops in Bavaria to render an oath of allegiance to the Bavarian
government. At that time the Democratic weekly Allgemeine
Zeitung was suppressed without warning because it had published
an appeal by the commander of the federal forces, General Hans
von Seeckt, to the Bavarian division. [144] While the radicals of
the right had smooth sailing, the radicals of the left were subjected to stringent repressions. All Communist newspapers were
suspended under the decree and severe punishment threatened for
printing, editing, storing, selling, distributing, or displaying
them. [145]

While the federal government was forced to admit its impotence toward Bavaria, it could and did proceed with vigor
against the Central German states of Saxony and Thuringia, which
were dominated by Socialist-Communist coalition governments.
Although at first sight the expediency, if not the equity, of such
unilateral application of emergency action is open to question,
the mutual interstimulation of rebellions from the left and from
the right in different parts of the country was an undeniable
fact. [146] By asserting its authority against one rebellious fac-
tion, the federal government would at the same time emerge
strengthened in its position against the other. The federal government was relieved of its difficulties when Hitler's Beer Hall
Putsch in November precipitated a schism between the monarchists and the National-Socialists.

The plight of the press throughout the Reich was further
aggravated by the transfer of the executive power to military
commanders. The result was a general leniency throughout the
country toward the rightist press and intransigence toward the
press of the left. [147] In fact, the army was repeatedly accused
by the left of attempting, under the cloak of emergency powers,
to influence political developments in Germany by bearing down
more heavily on the leftist press than the emergency situation
justified. [148]

While the emergency decree was in force, the judiciary
played a negligible role in relation to the press. Since the decree
did not provide for appeal to the ordinary courts, they came in
contact with the press only through the enforcement of the Protection Law. For reasons which have already been stated, it
is difficult, if not impossible, to unfold a comprehensive picture

of the judicial contribution to the precarious position of the press.
On the basis of the occasional published excerpts from court decisions it appears that the apprehensions concerning the political
reliability of the judiciary, which had partly motivated the enactment of special legislation, were justified. A comparison of the
decisions of the Federal Supreme Court and the Court of State
demonstrates the greater effectiveness of the latter in enforcing
the spirit of the Protection Law. Examples of Supreme Court
decisions include rulings that a vilification was punishable under
the Protection Law only if it was expressed in an especially rude
manner. [149] Yet, a reference to the Socialist ministers of Thuringia as thieves (Spitzbuben) was dismissed as inoffensive.
There can be little doubt that a decision such as this violated the
spirit of the Law, which was premised on the assumption that in
view of the authoritarian German tradition a derision of the
national symbols would perforce undermine the authority of the
republic. By contrast, the decisions of the Court of State reflected more accurately the spirit of the Law. [150] For example,
in the case of a Communist paper the Court based a conviction
for derision of the government on the general political tendency
of the newspaper. [151] Though this obvious discrimination may
elicit misgivings at first sight, it is actually quite compatible
with the extraordinary character of these special measures provoked by abnormal conditions. In view of the partisan affiliation
of many German newspapers, individual utterances attained a
special meaning in the light of the general attitude of a paper over
an extended period of time. For the same reason, the threat to
the republic implied in an utterance varied from paper to paper
and depended largely on the clientele at which it was directed.
Thus, a careless article in a Communist or National-Socialist
paper might precipitate serious disturbances, while the same article published in the moderate press might be without consequences. Apparently, the Court of State had recognized that the
extraordinary conditions of the period could not be dealt with in a
purely legalistic manner. Yet, the Court also had its less enlightened moments when it refused to assume jurisdiction over a
prepublication censorship established by a military commander
for new publications. [152]

On the whole neither the Court of State nor the Supreme
Court can with justice be accused of curtailing to any significant
extent the right of the press to criticize. If any generalization is
permissible on the basis of the scanty evidence available, a tendency toward unilateral leniency toward offenders of the right can
be discerned. The tenor of the court decisions suggests that this
tendency was more pronounced in the Supreme Court than in the
Court of State. Generally the judiciary manifested a rather stern
attitude when its Nationalist sensibilities were offended. A case

in point is the conviction of the Rote Fahne for libel because of a
reference to the ''cowardly retreat of 1918'' of the officers' corps
of the army, [153] although this remark could hardly be construed
as a threat to the security of the republic. This decision is in
striking contrast to that of a Berlin court imposing upon a rightist agitator a rather nominal fine of less than $100 for an article
demanding that the owners of German firms collaborating with
the French should be murdered, [154] in spite of the really acute
danger that such admonitions might result in concrete action.

Conclusions

The status of the press during this early turbulent period
did not offer an encouraging picture. Only rarely could the press
go about its business unmolested by the government. Most of the
time its freedom was defective on both the substantive and the
procedural level. Nevertheless, it is difficult to allocate any
specific blame for this predicament. The necessity for emergency measures cannot be denied. However, the instances in
which the government used its extraordinary powers to silence
criticism were extremely rare. Only in Bavaria were emergency powers used systematically and successfully to pursue the
political ends of its antirepublican government. The resulting
threat to the press was due largely to the congenital infirmities
of German federalism. In the absence of a clear-cut dualism
between federal and Land administrative authority, most of the
federal functions were performed by state and local agencies.
The predominance of Länder governments in case of conflict with
the Reich was therefore inevitable. The position of the Länder
was further strengthened by a clause of Article 48 of the federal
constitution permitting them to invoke dictatorial emergency
powers on their own initiative.

On the procedural side the press was not as well protected
as it might have been. The extent of judicial powers granted administrative agencies was not reassuring. The procedures were
gradually ameliorated by granting the right of appeal against confiscations and suppressions and requiring a statement of reasons
and time limits. Yet, the initial issuance of such orders and the
assumption of punitive powers by administrative agencies can
hardly inspire confidence.

While these institutional defects are easily discernible, the
real dilemma of the Weimar republic lay deeper. On the one
hand, drastic emergency measures, including the suspension of
the freedom of the press, were indispensable if the republic was
to survive. In every instance they were justifiable in terms of
the existing political tension. The fact that in actual practice

they were discriminatory against the left was the result of unfortunate political conditions and perhaps political blunders
rather than part of a conspiratorial grand design of Social Democrats and other republicans. In view of the initial strength of the
Social Democratic party it was perhaps neither necessary nor
wise for the government to rely on the support of professional
militarists as heavily as it did. It is quite conceivable that the
onslaughts from the extreme left could have been warded off by a
republican militia had the government chosen to build up such a
force. On the other hand, the continuous restrictions imposed
upon the press prevented the development of a free press and the
spirit of toleration without which such a freedom is not imaginable.
Since the preponderant tradition in Germany was antiliberal and
monarchic, any attempt to introduce a liberal system was doomed
as long as the very basis of the new form of government was subject to bitter disagreements among the citizenry. Even under a
liberal constitution and a genuine republican government, Germany was not only unable to implement the liberal guarantees but
was forced to adopt a decided partiality toward the antirepublican
right.

That the nature of the difficulty was not recognized appears
from the enactment of the emergency measures as a regular piece
of legislation. Administrative measures emphasizing efficiency
rather than justice[155] were no doubt better adapted to the requirements of the situation. Even granted that the strategy of
the right called for long-term arrangements, the wisdom of
making far-reaching restrictions of liberties part of the regular
law of the land within the context of a liberal constitution is
debatable. If temporally limited extraordinary measures are unable to restore political stability, the adequacy of liberal democracy as a system of government for such a society must itself
be doubted.

The failure of the men of Weimar to break radically with
the Empire tradition and the inability of the individual German
to adopt the liberal tradition have at times been held responsible
for the ineffectiveness of the institutional innovations.[156] The
experiences of the press provide abundant evidence to support
that contention. The measures taken against it bear a striking
resemblance to the imperial laws directed against insults to the
sovereign (Majestätsbeleidigung). However, it remains doubtful
whether a radical break with tradition is possible or even desirable. While the monarchy preceding the republic was firmly
grounded in tradition and provided the foundation for the concordia
of the citizens with reference to the fundamental aspects of that
system, no such social bond held the citizenry of the republic
together. The result was open hostility between republican and
monarchist Germans. Two different "nations" seemed to live

under one rule, a condition which brought Germany to the brink
of civil war. The opposition fought with violence and offered
resistance to the established political authority — methods quite
alien to German political mores. In its defense, the government
was forced to suspend the system of human rights from which it
derived its legitimacy. Conditions such as these constitute a
fragile basis on which to erect a system of toleration. Social
cohesion is a prerequisite for the operation of liberal principles.
They cannot be decreed with a stroke of the legislative pen; nor
will they acquire reality through a mere institutional formalism.

CHAPTER IV

THE PRESS AND THE COURTS, 1924-1930

Transition to Normalcy

When at the end of 1923 the Reichstag passed an enabling act conferring upon the Marx government extraordinary legislative powers for the purpose of alleviating the social and economic crisis, it appeared that the republic had weathered its most perilous storms. The stabilization of the currency had a soothing effect upon politically excited minds. Moreover, the Communists had decided not to attempt the violent overthrow of the republic for the time being. The abortive Hitler Putsch had brought the ideological cleavages between the factions of the extreme right into sharp focus, and when the showdown came, the conservatives supported the republic rather than Hitler. Moreover, in the early days of 1924 the local paramilitary organizations of the Social Democrats were consolidated into a republican defense organization on a national scale under the name of Reichsbanner Schwarz-Rot-Gold. The republican forces were thus in a better position to compete with the military establishments of the extreme left and the extreme right than at any time since the revolution.

The general political pacification enabled the government to lift the military state of emergency and return executive powers to the proper civilian authorities. [1] However, the general limitations imposed upon the press by the decree of September 26, 1923, were not repealed, although individual suppressions based on that decree were lifted. In most other respects the status of the press remained unchanged, since the minister of the interior was empowered to take all necessary steps for the prevention of an extraconstitutional change of the form of government, and for that purpose Article 118 of the Constitution was suspended. Moreover, the procedure for appeals against the suppression of newspapers provided for in the decree of September 26, 1923, remained in effect. The only changes were the repeal of restrictions imposed by the military and the transfer of responsibility for the maintenance of security to the civilian authorities. Consequently, a full-fledged state of emergency remained in existence as far as the press was concerned. [2] In fact, the already extensive powers of the federal government over the press were further broadened by a supplementary decree. [3] The clear-and-present-danger requirement, which had been implicit, in a rather diluted form to be sure, in the earlier decree, was

now wholly abandoned. Newspapers and periodicals could be
suppressed simply because they had incited to disobedience of
laws and administrative decrees or to violence against political
and economic opponents. The suppressions following the proclamation of the decree were severely criticized by virtually all
political parties. Especially outspoken were the objections of
the Social Democrats because of the vagueness and flexibility of
the new criteria. [4] The government justified its position in terms
of the recent agitation against the parties of the extreme right by
the Communist press, which had admonished its readers ''to beat
the fascists wherever they were encountered.'' This type of incitement, directed against hostile groups rather than against the
government, had not been dealt with by the earlier decree. Obviously, the government could not stand by idly while the violent
struggle among radical groups threatened to disrupt the cohesion
of society. Only through comprehensive and flexible emergency
powers, it was contended, could the spirit of revolution, class
struggle, and open violence be prevented from disturbing public
order. [5] The argument of the government was a persuasive one.
Surely, unless it could monopolize the legitimate use of force and
ensure peaceful settlement of political differences, it had lost its
raison d'être. No constitution can serve any useful purpose if
competing groups are permitted to settle their differences through
resort to violence. Failure to aim violent action at the government proper did not detract from the seriousness of the situation.
In fact, the new strategy mapped out by the extreme right, which
eventually induced the downfall of the republic, aimed only indirectly at the violent overthrow of the government. Its primary
target was the constitutional order itself. If through violent fac-
tional strife the inability of the constitutional authorities to maintain the internal peace could be demonstrated, then the constitutional order would collapse almost automatically without neces-
sitating resort to open violence.

It was not long before controls over the press were relaxed.
The existing social, economic, and political tensions, which had
been reduced by the stabilization of the currency, were further
eased through foreign loans made available, mostly by the United
States, under the provisions of the Dawes Plan. It was quite apparent to German political leaders that America was not likely to
make extensive investments in a country torn by internal strife.
The two capitalistic parties of the right, the moderate People's
party and the more extreme Nationalist party, were thus induced
to accept, or at least tolerate, the republic. Consequently, the
Nationalist party lost its character as an opposition party and
joined the governmental coalition. As a further result the enabling act was abolished, the state of emergency lifted, and the
Reichstag repossessed of its constitutional powers. However,

not all factions of the Nationalist party had reconciled themselves
to the republican government. While the impetus to cooperation
emanated from industrialists and big merchants, intellectuals,
civil servants, army officers, and landowners continued their
former hostility. [6]

     After the enabling act and the state of emergency were
lifted, the press remained subject only to the restrictions of the
Protection Law, which was to remain in effect until 1927. These
restrictions were temporarily relaxed during the period of the
first plebiscitary presidential election in 1925, when all prohibition orders of newspapers then in effect were suspended. But
even then, the Communists contended that wholesale suppressions
of Communist papers had taken place shortly before and after the
election in various parts of the Reich, not excluding areas in
which the Social Democrats were in control. [7] Furthermore, the
offices of Communist newspapers were allegedly searched and
propaganda material distinctly designed for the presidential election campaign confiscated. [8] The government claimed to have dis-
covered a wealth of treasonable material, which was immediately
examined and returned to the Communist party upon court orders. [9]
The numerous suppressions of Communist newspapers were explained in terms of their continued incitement to violence. [10]

     The restrictions contained in the Protection Law could not
be seriously objected to by the responsible press. Considerable
latitude in criticizing existing conditions and propagating political
ideas was conceded even to extremist parties. Nevertheless,
both the Communist and the National-Socialist parties urged the
repeal of the Law, since it forced more self-restraint upon their
press than they considered compatible with their strategy. Their
aspirations would come to naught unless their strategy was supported by violent action. The requisite emotional appeals to the
masses would certainly bring them in conflict with the Protection
Law. Even the Social Democrats, though favoring the continuation
of the Law as a means of combating the rightist murder organizations, [11] were highly critical of the manner in which it had been
enforced. In the hands of a rightist judiciary it had become a tool
directed unilaterally against the left while flagrant violations of
the right remained frequently unpunished. [12] The eventual relaxation of the Law[13] was perhaps the result of these pressures as
well as of the general political pacification. The Protection Law,
which was to expire in 1927, was nonetheless extended for a two-
year period with the support of the Nationalist party, [14] which
since the enactment of the law had exchanged its opposition for
participation in the governmental coalition. Moreover, it had been
forced to relinquish its former monopoly on the rightist opposition
to the National Socialists. The extension law[15] took one further
step toward a return to normalcy by transferring the jurisdictions

of the Court of State to the Federal Administrative Court, which
was contemplated but not as yet established; in the meantime
jurisdiction was to be assumed by one of the senates of the Supreme Court. This was generally interpreted as a concession
to the right, which had never ceased to regard the Court of State
as an extraordinary court in the nature of a revolutionary
tribunal.

The Courts and the Protection Law

The press delicts arising under the Protection Law consisted essentially of two types: (1) vilification of the constitutionally determined republican form of government or its representatives; (2) incitement to a violent change in the form of
government. The published court decisions indicate a predominance of rightist offenders in the first category and of Communist
offenders in the second. The reasons for this phenomenon are
suggested by the different strategies of the two parties. The right
tried to bring about the downfall of the republic by undermining
its prestige; the left attempted to prepare its violent overthrow by
exploiting existing dissatisfaction and social unrest. As in the
previous period, decisions in the first category were marked by
an extraordinary leniency, of which the rightist press was the
main beneficiary. Generally, sincere political criticism was
permitted full scope. To be sure, such references to members
of the government as "tribunes of the gutter anxious for positions,"
or as "the vultures of 1918," were properly held a violation of
the law. [16] However, these rather extreme cases were counterbalanced by an impressive array of lenient decisions. A case in
point is a decision of a lower court in Berlin acquitting the editor of the Deutsche Zeitung, which had referred to the republic
as "the slimy and slippery democratic republic which, to the
misfortune of the German people, had prepared Germany's fu-
neral."[17] In this and many similar cases the court found a basis
for extenuating circumstances in the sharp political fight conducted through the press, in the fact that the vilification was not
especially rude and that it was not aimed directly at governmental
officials but indirectly at the system. [18]

The verdicts of the courts in cases involving seditionist activities or preparation to sedition, which were punishable under
the Protection Law as well as under the general penal code, [19]
reveal an entirely different picture. The Communists, who were
primarily involved in these cases, were thus placed in an un-
favorable position as compared with their rightist counterparts.
In fact, the antiseditionist provisions eventually became a powerful
weapon against the Communists in the hands of the judiciary. [20]

The threat to the security of the republic inherent in seditionist publications is, of course, undeniable. Yet, the actual danger could have been determined only in terms of the objective stability of the republic as a measure of clear and present danger. Not only was such an evaluation wholly lacking, but the courts frequently established criminality subjectively in terms of intent. While the ease with which the sedition laws were applied was cause for concern, the adverse action of the courts was perhaps justifiable in the case of an editor of a Communist party newspaper, who was sentenced to six months in jail for two articles published in his absence, [21] and in relation to book-distribution agencies operated by political parties for party purposes. [22] Of a more serious nature was the application of sedition laws to printers, typesetters, and messengers on the assumption that they must have known the contents of the publication. [23] In defense of its action the Court contended that the individuals concerned were not sentenced in their capacity as bookdealers, printers, messengers, etc., but rather as officials of the Communist party, an organization hostile to the existing order and determined to overthrow it. Consequently, every promotion of its aims, even if purely literary in form, was to be regarded as preparation for "high treason" (sedition). [24] The logic of that view is doubtful. First, the almost indiscriminate sentencing of individuals connected in a merely technical capacity with the production and distribution of the propaganda of a legal party was bound to have an unduly intimidating and restrictive effect. Secondly, the stability of the republic at that time as well as the temporary abolition of revolutionary activities by international communism hardly justified such drastic measures. The fatuity of the court's reasoning was demonstrated even more clearly when it sentenced the editor of a bulletin published by the parliamentary Communist party for "high treason" because it included a speech by the Communist representative Ernst Thaelmann delivered in the Reichstag. The treasonable fact presumably lay in the reproduction of the speech separately from all other speeches delivered during that session. It therefore failed to meet the standard of a literal transcription of the debates, [25] which would have been entitled to constitutional protection.

The Courts and the General Treason Laws

The most notable change in the methods of the political struggle during this relatively stable period was the recognition by the right of the futility of violence for the overthrow of the republic and the resulting substitution of nonviolent agitation for violent action. [26] This shift of emphasis in the over-all strategy

did not mean the immediate abandonment of all plans for violent
action. While plans for the assassination of Gustav Stresemann
and the erection of a dictatorship, contrived by the president of
the Pan-German League, Heinrich Class, still existed, they
were frustrated before they had had an opportunity to concretize.
The democratic republic had finally consolidated its forces sufficiently to protect itself against violent action. The period from
1926 on therefore signaled the end of violent threats against the
government. However, the outward appearance of calm and stability was deceptive. It is no exaggeration to state that the old
political and social cleavages had not lost in sharpness and that
Germany was no closer to a genuine reconciliation on the basis
of the democratic republic. In fact, later developments clearly
demonstrated that the rightist opposition had not given up hope of
liquidating it. [27] Yet, for the time being the prospects of the
republic seemed promising. It had built up a reliable militia of
its own; foreign credits had facilitated a desperately needed
economic reconstruction. It is therefore not to be wondered at
that the political agencies of the government assumed a less indulgent attitude toward the right than heretofore, even though
the Nationalist party was now a member of the governmental
coalition. The fact of the matter is that, when the right relin-
quished its violent method, the government became increasingly
sensitive to parliamentary and extraparliamentary criticism by
the numerically strong Social Democrats, who constituted a
formidable opposition. Under these changed conditions the right
could derive comfort from the decisions of the courts. The
judiciary, still largely staffed by imperial judges of a conservative bent of mind, jumped in to carry on the fight against the left
and to prevent the republic from entrenching itself too firmly.
The main target of the judicial attack was the press of the left
since it was the medium par excellence for the diffusion of republican ideas. To accomplish their purpose, the courts availed
themselves of a device which had suggested itself earlier in the
Fechenbach trial: the concept of treason committed by the press
(Landesverrat begangen durch die Presse) as an offense against
the general penal code (Section 92, StGB). The application of the
penal provisions, which frequently bordered on absurdity, proved
an extraordinarily effective method for filling the gaps left by the
penal provisions for "high treason" (Hochverrat).

The pertinent provisions of the penal code (Section 92, StGB)
simply stipulated that: "Whoever willfully passes on to another
government, or announces publicly, information concerning secrets of state or plans of fortifications [Festungspläne] or such
documents, dossiers, or news of which he knows that their secre-
cy toward another government is necessary in the interest of
the German Reich or one of its states, will be sentenced to no less

than two years in the penitentiary. '' There can be little doubt that
the application of this provision to the leftist press was responsible for the enormous increase in the number of prosecutions
for Landesverrat during this period. [28] In the vast majority of
cases the press was neither accused nor convicted of betraying
military or diplomatic secrets of state to foreign governments.
Rather, the punishable act consisted in calling the attention of
the German authorities and the public to the illegal activities of
secret paramilitary organizations which were preparing the overthrow of the republic. [29] By this standard a newspaper could be
convicted of treason because it had disclosed the existence of
conditions, illegal under German law, for the purpose of stimu-
lating remedial action. Publications mostly affected by the
ruling were the leftist and pacifist press, which disclosed regu-
larly details of organization and armaments of rightist secret
organizations or of illegal activities of the army officered primarily by persons of antirepublican sentiment. The fact that
frequently much or all of this information had previously been
common knowledge in foreign countries had no mitigating effects
on the decisions of the courts. [30] The two causes célèbres in the
long series of press trials were those involving the Weltbühne
and Das Andere Deutschland. In the first case, both the author
and the editor, Carl von Ossietzky, were sentenced by the Supreme Court to eighteen months' imprisonment because of an
article objecting to the maintenance of a mysterious section
''M'' of the army, which allegedly operated aircraft not authorized by the Treaty of Versailles. Actually, the matter had been
publicized well before the publication of the Weltbühne article in
1929 through an interpellation of the war minister in the Reichstag by the Social Democratic party. [31] However, the government
charged that the article had "alluded more precisely to a secret
military air force section than the parliamentary proceedings
had. '' If this tortuous reasoning seems rather perplexing from
the point of view of logic, it is more comprehensible if viewed
in terms of its motivation. The actual reason for the conviction
apparently was the desire of the minister of war, Wilhelm Groener,
to silence an annoying critic, who had embarrassed the army on
previous occasions, and in this endeavor he enjoyed the support
of the courts. The Weltbühne had made itself especially un-
popular in military circles when it published articles in defense
of a certain Lieutenant Paul Schulz, who was sentenced to death
because of a number of Vehme murders he had committed in the
schwarze Reichswehr. The Weltbühne contended that Schulz had
been merely a tool of the real culprits, Colonel von Bock, Colonel
Kurt von Schleicher, and General Seeckt, on whose orders he had
acted. On the basis of these articles Ossietzky was tried for
Landesverrat and convicted, but subsequently acquitted by the

court of appeal. However, in the case of the "air secrets"
Groener succeeded in immobilizing his critic at least temporarily. The obvious inconsistency in the position of the government did not disconcert the court to any visible degree. On the
one hand, Ossietzky was accused of having revealed military
secrets; on the other, the existence of the air force unit in
question was denied. How could the accused reveal secrets if
the subjects of such alleged secrets were mere figments of
imagination? Was not his conviction an implied admission that
the government had violated its treaty obligations?[32]

The other cause célèbre involving Das Andere Deutschland
ended in a sentence for both editor and author of an objectionable
article to a prison term of nine months each.[33] The article in
question had asserted that, declarations of the chancellor and
minister of war to the contrary notwithstanding, the temporary
volunteers recruited by the army during the state of emergency
of 1923-1924 had not been discharged after its termination in
clear violation of the obligations of the Treaty of Versailles. The
Court based its conviction on the assertion that the purpose of the
article had not been to call the attention of the government to illegal conditions for the sake of remedying them. Rather, the
author had accused the government of tolerating and favoring such
conditions, leaving Germany exposed to international action for
treaty violation. The Court allowed that such information might
have been brought directly to the attention of the responsible
authorities or the Reichstag. Actually, such a course of action
was not without hazards. Information of this nature submitted to
governmental authority, especially the ministry of war, frequently resulted in the prosecution of the informant rather than
the accused.[34] It was also unlikely that such information reported to the Reichstag would result in action unless backed up by
public-opinion pressure. However, the conditions were not likely
to come to the attention of the public if the press was silenced
through intimidation.

Paradoxically, the trials of the press served to shield seditionist activities. The criminal provisions against sedition and
treason were actually supplementary in intent and meaning, the
one protecting the state against internal, the other against external, threats. However, in the interpretation given by the courts,
the disclosure by the press of seditionist activities designed to
protect the state was punishable as treason.[35] Thus, the two provisions equally designed for the protection of the state had become
mutually exclusive. The press had to remain silent when it un-
earthed sedition unless it was willing to run the risk of an indictment for treason. It has been contended that this practice of the
courts was part of a well-thought-out system which would furnish
a weapon for a future intensification of the class struggle, since

the bourgeoisie felt more threatened by the internal than by the
external enemy. [36] Regardless of whether or not this interpretation had a basis in reality, the intimidation of the leftist press
was so effective in fact that the illegal rightist organizations
could carry on their subversive activities without having to be
concerned with the possibility of embarrassing publicity. Conviction for treason (Landesverrat) had become a routine opera-
tional risk for editors of newspapers. The plight of the press
was not alleviated by the fact that out of eighty-five prosecutions
only one ended in conviction. [37] On the contrary, the abnormal
proportion of convictions to the number of prosecutions indicates
the degree of irresponsibility and ease with which prosecutions
were undertaken, adding substantially to the fears and insecurity
of the press in view of the increasing unpredictability of the consequences of their work. The situation is well characterized by
the statistics of Landesverrat given by E. J. Gumbel:[38]

Reports on violations received	360
Disregarded	45
Prosecuted	315
Suspended by the federal prosecutor	252
Still in process	60
Convictions	3

These figures do not include sedition (Hochverrat) and espionage
committed by the press. In spite of the rare convictions the
nationalist attempt to intimidate the leftist and pacifist press was
singularly successful. Journalists were hesitant to run the risk
of being stigmatized as traitors to their country. The greatly
reduced frequency of such prosecutions after 1927 indicates perhaps the success of these attempts to silence the leftist press.
A measure of their success was the consolidation of Nationalist
forces, furthered by the silencing of the press, which enabled
them to use overt, rather than secret, paramilitary organizations
for the attainment of their ends. The rather substantial losses
of the Nationalists and National-Socialists in the general election
of 1928, and the correlative gains of the parties of the center and
the left, are not necessarily reliable indicators of the declining
effectiveness of the right. The temporary recovery of the pro-
republican forces can easily be explained in terms of the general
economic prosperity which had been on the increase in Germany
ever since 1924 as well as of the restoration of the country's
international status. However, electoral success in time of relative economic stability is hardly sufficient to inspire much confidence concerning the security of a democratic government until
it has demonstrated its capability to survive severe crises. The
temporary electoral setback of the right surely was less significant

than the militancy of a relentless and well-organized National-
Socialist party upholding "the ideal of a new and better state of
the future."[39] A professional and ever ready oppositional group
devoted to the attainment of its ends by whatever means could
easily be converted into an effective revolutionary striking force
even though its membership was limited to a relatively small number.

An attempt to plug the remaining loopholes in the Nationalist
methods of subversion was made in connection with an abortive
attempt to reform the penal code in 1926 and 1927. This reform,
if adopted, would have vastly increased the range of punishable
press activities.[40] The draft, submitted by the Nationalist party,
provided that disclosure of information detrimental to Germany's
international position was punishable as treason regardless of
whether or not it had any basis in fact. This would have saved the
government the embarrassment of the Ossietzky case. Moreover,
the draft introduced the novel notion of treasonable breach of faith
(landesverräterische Untreue) to protect the interest of Reich and
Länder. Thereby information passed on loyally to the federal
government concerning disaffection of a state government or, for
example, of a Bavarian general of the federal armed force might
have resulted in a sentence of up to fifteen years' confinement in
a penitentiary. That this provision would have spelled the dissolution of the federal union is too obvious to require elaboration.
A further, rather bizarre, provision was the prohibition to pass
on information endangering the welfare of the Reich or a Land
to any other individual even if he was a member of the Reichstag.
Although the reform code was never enacted, it elicits considerable interest, since it reveals clearly the strategy pursued by the
rightists in their attempt to subvert the republic.

Conclusions

The difficulties of the press during this period of stability
were essentially different from those which had confronted it during
the early turbulent years. For the first time since the inception
of the republic could it operate unimpeded by emergency decrees
or discriminatory legislation after the decrees of September, 1923,
and February, 1924, had been rescinded. The only remaining
special restraints were those embodied in the Protection Law of
1922, which, however, were sufficiently moderate to serve as a
reasonable general standard of conduct for the press. The only
feature indicating its extraordinary character was the substitution
of administrative for judicial sanctions. Yet, the marked bias of
the judiciary made administrative action appear preferable. It
may seem strange at first sight that the Protection Law remained

in force throughout this period of general political pacification. However, the deceptive nature of the stability is difficult to overemphasize. The continued existence of the republic still was by no means a foregone conclusion. The transfer of judicial authority to the administration notwithstanding, the courts retained considerable power in relation to the press, since the most devastating attack did not fall within the scope of the Protection Law but of the general sedition laws.

The victims of the frequent judicial encroachments upon the freedom of the press were the publications of the left. Relying on the judiciary, the rightist parties, participating in the governmental coalition, could carry on their fight against the left without endangering that collaboration through political action in the form of special decrees and laws. While such measures promoted by republican forces in the past had tended to minimize the antirepublican judicial influence, the possibility of perpetuating the republican spirit had now become wholly illusory. The suppression of the freedom of the press at a time when the general political stability would have permitted a high degree of liberty was a remarkable achievement of judicial genius. Its actions could hardly be justified in terms of the Communist threat. The Communist party had reached its peak in the election of 1924. It had declined steadily ever since. An intermediate recovery of its voting strength still left it considerably short of its record strength of 1924, so that the conclusion of an imminent Communist threat was definitely without basis. The Social Democrats, staunch supporters of the republic, also had gained considerably at the expense of the right. The sedition laws would have been quite effective to cope with any potential Communist threat. There was little justification for invoking treason laws. The actual motivation of the rightist judiciary apparently was the desire to strike a blow at leftists and pacifists in general. That could be done only through treason laws, since their loyal support of the republic rendered the non-Communist left immune against sedition laws.

The grave responsibility of the German judiciary for the suppression of liberties is undeniable. It is easy to comprehend that the tender sprouts of a rising liberalism could not expand in the frigid atmosphere which the courts had created. Only where the liberal spirit has already taken firm root in a people's tradition will suppression elicit resistance and enhance the liberal cause. In its absence, the denial of constitutional rights inevitably results in disillusionment and open hostility to liberalism itself. The German courts, part and parcel of a predominantly illiberal environment, did an effective job in disparaging constitutionalism. The republican forces were powerless to cope with these conditions. Volitional acts and positive institutions could

be of little avail unless the ideals were deeply engraved in the
hearts of people. Without such firmly established ideals the
vicious circle of denials of liberties and the resulting disparagement of these ideals seems inevitable.

The judicial strategy of turning political laws, designed to
protect the republic, against the republican as well as antirepublican left while granting the full benefit of constitutional
protection to the counterrevolutionary right was a masterpiece of
political craftsmanship. However, not all judicial action pointing
in that direction can be regarded as part of a comprehensive
sinister design to stamp out leftism of any kind. It cannot with
justice be denied that to some extent the reasons for the apparent
discrimination against the left were beyond the control of the
courts. The discrepancies in the judicial treatment of rightist
and leftist radicalism was to a large measure inherent in the logic
of the situation. Communist strategy was severely handicapped
by its ideological commitment to the pursuit of the class struggle.
The improbability of winning an electoral majority on a platform
of national disunity forced the Communists to renounce genuine
parliamentary co-operation in favor of the militant methods of
the street. Little judicial ingenuity was required to curb the activities of such a movement, constitutional guarantees notwithstanding.

The National-Socialist movement, on the other hand,
operated more skillfully and availed itself of more subtle methods. Masquerading under the guise of a party of the right, it
could count on the support of most rightists, who did not take the
trouble to subject it to an analysis which might have revealed its
true revolutionary character. After the abortive Beer Hall Putsch
it had come to realize the futility of forcible attempts to seize
governmental power. This view had gained in persuasiveness,
since the seizure of power through "legal means," that is, through
obtaining a parliamentary majority, was a distinct possibility.
Therefore, National-Socialist attacks upon the government were
relatively mild if compared with Communist agitation. Their primary aim was to create dissension within the population which
would force the government to abandon its governing function.
Their victims were such groups as were considered unlikely can-
didates for conversion. Their attacks upon the government, while
effective, were so vague that they could only with difficulty be
brought within the four corners of the laws and decrees for the
protection of the republic. Such methods were hard to assail. The
difficulty was further increased by the fact that the activism of the
radical parties was not essentially unique. The republican parties
had equally exploited the mass emotionalism of the street at the
expense of the relatively rational atmosphere of the assembly hall.
If any difference in the tactics of radical and republican parties

existed at all, it was one of degree. Were the courts, then, to be expected to deny means of agitation to one party which could be employed with impunity by others? National-Socialist strategy had the further advantage of relying primarily on the positive dissemination of inherently antidemocratic doctrines, which relieved them of the necessity of disparaging the republic through direct vilification. [41] This does not mean that the Nazis abstained from such vilification; it is merely to indicate that it was a less indispensable facet of their strategy than of the strategy of the Communists. Hence the more elusive nature of National-Socialist agitation. Considerable following could therefore be attracted through the mere diffusion of its antidemocratic doctrines.

In view of these novel strategies, which could no longer be effectively combated through the antiquated protection laws, effective judicial action against the extreme right was far from being an easy task. Yet, the difficulty was not insurmountable. Had the courts struck down consistently and courageously the violations of the law by National-Socialists wherever possible, the effectiveness of their strategy could certainly have been minimized. However, mistaking the party for a conservative movement of the right and nationalistic rowdyism for patriotism, the judiciary was not imbued with the desire to curb National-Socialist activism. A splendid opportunity for the republic to give a demonstration of the blessings of responsibly used freedoms was thus lost.

CHAPTER V

THE PRESS IN A PERIOD OF ECONOMIC INSTABILITY, 1930-1933

Economic Difficulties and the Re-enactment of the Law for the Protection of the Republic

Hopes that the pacification of Germany's political life would be a lasting one and eventually permit the formation of a firm constitutional basis for the republic proved illusory. The results of the general election of 1928, which brought the Social Democratic party back into the governmental coalition as a leading participant, merely disguised the essentially unstable political situation. The stability of the republic depended in the last analysis on two primary factors: economic well-being and the support of the army. To ensure the first requirement, the government depended on foreign loans, for the attainment of which the financiers were instrumental; for the latter it needed the support of the generals. In spite of their seeming co-operation, neither financiers nor generals had really acquiesced in the republic as a lasting form of government for Germany. The first signs of the political fragility of the republic appeared in the spring of 1929. Growing unemployment and budgetary difficulties of the federal government were foreshadowing the world economic crisis which was to have especially disastrous effects upon German politics. At this time the National-Socialists received ideological reassurances through a schism within the Nationalist party. The right wing of that party under the leadership of Alfred Hugenberg divorced itself from the collaborationist policy of the moderate elements and proclaimed an intransigent political program. The secession of this group had vastly greater political effects than its unimpressive numerical strength seemed to warrant. In conjunction with the National Socialists they had enough weight to render the already tenuous political balance of the republic even more precarious. Their increasing self-confidence in the light of the misfortunes of the republican government induced the National-Socialists further to undermine its shaky foundations through a strategy of violence against their adversaries. At the opposite pole, the Communists abandoned their pacific course, which had been imposed upon them by Moscow since 1924, for more radical methods of political action. [1] The new strategy precipitated violent clashes with the police. Historians are nonetheless agreed that the Communist party neither intended to embark upon a path of open revolutionary action nor was vigorous enough to carry it out had such a plan existed. [2] In fact,

a last open clash between Communists and police had occurred in
Berlin on May 1, 1929, as a result of a refusal by the police to
relax a general prohibition of demonstrations on the first of May.
The incident was limited in scope and certainly not to be regarded
as an overture for a general revolution. [3]

It was in these circumstances that the Law for the Protection
of the Republic was due to expire. In view of the intense political
agitation and the increasing resort to violence by the extremist
parties for the settlement of their political differences, the government tried to obtain an extension of the law. The attempt miscarried as a result of the joint opposition of Communists, right-
wing Nationalists, and National-Socialists. [4] The Nationalists
expressed their customary apprehensions that a law of this type
served to stifle any criticism of the government. The Communists
did not object so much to the provisions of the Law as to their unilateral application against the left in the past. [5] It was also charged
that the Law had permitted wholesale suppression of Communist
publications on the basis of their general political attitude rather
than because of specific violations. [6]

The government could not acquiesce in the decision to let the
Protection Law expire. The steadily growing unemployment combined with financial difficulties created by the business recession
tended to encourage the antirepublican spirit at both poles. Little
comfort was to be derived from the change in revolutionary methods of the extremist parties which spared the republic from direct
attacks. Especially the extreme right had been impressed with the
failure of its earlier revolutionary attempts and with the apparent
consolidation of the republic. It appeared that resort to devious
methods might be a more promising approach for the attainment of
the desired end than direct attacks upon the republic. The Communists, perhaps because of their unswerving faith in the class
struggle as the basic political driving force, seemed to be less
adroit in adapting their methods to changed circumstances. Their
loss of revolutionary drive was probably due primarily to the
vacillating policy of Moscow, which was moving its Communist
pawns abroad in accordance with the requirements of Soviet Russia's
national policy. Consequently, neither the right nor the left any
longer contemplated seriously the destruction of the constitutional
order through direct and open force. The change in subversive
technique — which had presented difficulties of enforcement previously and was now developed into a system — caused both to
carry on their fight under the disguise of legitimate political parties seemingly competing with other parties within the context of
the constitutional order. Thus they could claim the full protection
of constitutional liberties for themselves. Democratic society, it
was realized, could be more effectively disrupted by inciting the
masses to violence, not against the government, but against their

political opponents. The result would no doubt be a clear demonstration of the impotence of the government to maintain or restore order. The inevitable consequence would be a loss of confidence of the people in the efficacy of their government and thereby facilitate the seizure of power by extremists through constitutional means.[7] The press was assigned a role of primary importance in that scheme. It was ideally suited to incite the masses to wage a fraternal war against their opponents. At the same time, the radical parties would inescapably be the beneficiaries of the involuntary publicity given them by the republican press, which reported at length on their turbulent activities.[8] The previous strategy of intimidating outstanding representatives of the republic was abandoned in favor of the new and more elusive technique of intimidating the masses of the citizens and showing up the weakness of the republican government.

The new direction of subversive strategy convinced the government of an overwhelming need for the re-establishment of the expired Protection Law. Eventually a new Law for the Protection of the Republic, which was to remain in force until December 31, 1932,[9] was enacted over the objections of the left and the right. In the light of existing conditions the act was unassailable. The steadily rising number of unemployed constituted a political reserve army readily available for recruitment by any radical movement, right or left. This revolutionary potential was progressively activated by the flagrant transgressions of journalistic privileges by the radical press. To counteract the provocation of the masses and prevent the impression that even minor acts of violence would cause the entire fabric of the republic to fall apart was the undeniable duty of the government. The very real need for governmental action was amply demonstrated by the numerous inflammatory publications in the Communist and National-Socialist press. The former were aiming to arouse their clientele by pointing to the presumably imminent dawn of the revolutionary era; the latter were attempting to promote their cause by further disrupting the already precarious social cohesion through increased attacks upon such groups as the Catholic Church and the Jews, who were blamed for all of Germany's ills and for employing the republic for their own selfish ends.

The need for the new Protection Law could not with justice be minimized through reference to the remoteness of an overt attempt at violent overthrow of the constitutional order. The consolidation of republican defenses could hardly be taken as a reliable gauge of its political stability. If the disruptive agitation of the radical parties could thwart the formation of a working majority in the Reichstag, the republic was doomed and political authority would fall into the lap of one of the radical movements like a ripe plum. At the same time, the novel strategy was virtually immune against

legal repression, since the republic itself was not under direct
fire. Hence, the radical parties could not be easily denied the protection of the bill of rights. Since the new revolutionary strategy
relied heavily on propaganda aimed at the vast masses of people,
no attempt to curb political rowdyism could be effective unless it
restricted journalistic excesses. The measures taken were fully
vindicated by the events of the last years of the republic, which
signaled the final break in the leftist front and the irreconcilable
hostility of the Communists to the parliamentary republic. The
acceptance of that challenge by the government was clearly indicated by its promise, made during the debates surrounding the
enactment of the Protection Law, of the equal application of its
sanctions to all violators regardless of their political coloration.[10]
The wisdom of the government's failure to restore leftist solidarity, which had permitted some rays of hope to break through the
political clouds of 1922, may at first sight appear dubious. Only
a solid front of the left would have been able to checkmate the increasing antirepublican stirrings of the right. Yet, upon closer
scrutiny such an attempt hardly appeared feasible. The rather
tenuous governmental coalition encompassed bourgeois parties as
far to the right as the German-National People's Party (DNVP).
The latter was not likely to support a bill which was primarily directed against rightist offenders. A leftist coalition, even if one
were to indulge in dreams of a possible collaboration between Communists, Social Democrats, and Democrats, would have fallen
short of a parliamentary majority. However, in reality any such
coalition would have been illusory because of the ideological handi-
caps restraining the freedom of action of the Communists. The
Marxist-Communist catechism exalted the destruction of the social-
democratic republic over the fight against fascism. An even more
disastrous ideological obstacle to co-operation was the addition of
fascism to the Marxian dialectical ladder as a final phase of capitalism through which historical evolution would inevitably have to [11]
pass before the predetermined revolutionary collapse could occur.
A theoretical construction such as this admitted of only one conclusion, which guided the actions of the German Communists to the
bitter end: to enable history to pursue its predetermined course
the destruction of the republic was the immediate goal even if its
attainment required temporary support of the National-Socialist
rise to power. The Marxian revolutionary time schedule buttressed
their optimistic confidence that the Hitler movement could not possibly maintain itself in power for any length of time.

     In its provisions affecting the press, the new law drew the
permissible limits of press activity somewhat narrower than the old
law in spite of their essential similarity. The most conspicuous
change was the extension of the provisions concerning vilification
of the form of government and its outstanding representatives. The

leniency of the courts in cases where the derogatory utterance had
not been expressed in an especially rude manner had provoked
considerable popular dissatisfaction. The problem confronting the
legislators, then, was one of broadening the criteria of vilification
sufficiently to make the protection of the republic effective without
at the same time curbing sharp and factual criticism of the government. [12] It was believed that this end could be attained by formu-
lating the offense after the pattern of the crimen laesae maiestatis
of imperial Germany. The criminal offense was now extended to
include "malicious and premeditated derision" ("wer. . .
böswillig und mit Überlegung verächtlich macht"). [13] In this manner vilification was made more inclusive but was qualified by the
subjective criteria of "maliciousness" and "premeditation. " The
flag was protected against the same offenses for similar reasons.
References to the colors of the republic as "black-red-egg-yolk-
yellow" or as a "Jew-flag" had previously remained unpunished.
Vilification of the colors did as much to undermine the republic as
that of the form of government and its representatives. Moreover,
the protection of the reputation of deceased presidents of the Reich
or ministers of Reich and Länder was extended to those having died
a natural death regardless of whether they had died in office or
after. [14] A new provision made incitement to, and approval or
glorification of, acts of violence for political reasons a punishable
offense. The provisions aiming specifically at the press extended
administrative confiscation and suppression of newspapers and
periodicals to violations of the penal code in regard to sedition
(Sections 81-86, StGB) and incitement to disobedience of the laws
(Section 110, StGB). This further extension of nonjudicial confiscation and suppression may appear surprising at first sight in view
of the shift of the governmental coalition to the right. This strange
phenomenon can perhaps be explained in terms of the traditionally
higher respect of the Germans for administrative than for judicial
authorities. It may also have been due to the fact that key positions
in the administrative services were now well-staffed by Nationalists. The Court of State was not revived. The functions formerly
performed by that tribunal were now assigned to the Supreme Administrative Court or, pending its establishment, to the Supreme
Court.

The justification of special legislation under the prevailing
conditions is apparent. Although the new law restricted the press
more severely than its predecessor, it did not muzzle full criticism
of the government, its representatives, and its symbols. It attempted to impose restraints upon the form, rather than the substance, of critical utterances and check the gross distortion of facts
which had become common journalistic practice at the time.

ECONOMIC INSTABILITY

Eclipse of Constitutionalism and the Freedom of the Press

The Brüning Régime

As the global economic crisis mounted and foreign credits
were withdrawn from Germany, political tension and agitation
against the republic increased. Since the radical parties had re-
linquished their overt insurrectionist designs, the political struggle was now carried on in the streets against opponents and in the
Reichstag, where the rapidly growing number of radical representatives became progressively less willing to co-operate, thereby
causing a legislative paralysis. The impotence of the Reichstag
was part and parcel of the over-all strategy designed to win over
the masses, who could facilitate seizure of power by means of an
electoral victory. Under the strain of the economic crisis radical
mass appeal increased in proportion to the inability of the Reichstag to function. At the same time, the growth of the radical representation in the Reichstag rendered that body less capable of
functioning as a policy maker. The vital role of the press in supporting that strategy, which was directed at the creation and maintenance of mass emotionalism at high pitch, is apparent. Hence,
curbing journalistic irresponsibility remained a problem of first
magnitude which the government could not ignore without being remiss in its paramount obligations. One of the main difficulties was
posed by the fact that most of the responsible editors of radical
papers enjoyed parliamentary immunity as members of the Reichstag or of state legislatures. In the spring of 1931 most of the four
hundred cases against the press had to be suspended because of such
immunities. Consequently, one of the most important activities
disrupting the republic could not be curbed.[15]

By late 1930 the mutual violent attacks by the radical parties
upon their political opponents had become a regular Sunday activity.
The National-Socialists indulged primarily in excesses against Jews
and the smashing of windows of large department stores in the major
cities. The Communists contributed their share by provoking weekly battles with the National-Socialists. The main victim of this
strife was the republic. The general public violence was further
aroused by the clamoring of the Nationalist paramilitary organization Stahlhelm for a re-election of the Prussian assembly. In the
course of the political battles ensuing in this connection the number
of political murders reached unprecedented heights.[16] The main
beneficiaries of this systematized chaos were the National-Socialists. The challenge could be met only through more stringent
measures of control.

The Brüning regime launched its offensive against political
radicalism early in 1931 with the issuance of an emergency decree

"to battle political excesses. "[17] The most rigorous new restrictions referred to posters and handbills, while the restrictions for
newspapers and periodicals were somewhat less severe. Confiscation and suppression was now authorized in the event of incitement to disobedience of the laws or of vilification or malicious
derision of organs, institutions, authorities, or leading officials
of the state, or of religious communities having corporative status,
their institutions, customs or symbols of worship. Moreover, the
time limit for suppressions was now extended to eight weeks for
daily papers. Original jurisdiction over confiscations and suppressions was vested in the local police authorities, whose decisions
could be ultimately appealed to the Supreme Court if the police
orders were not reversed by higher administrative organs. While
the freedom of the press was thereby further restricted, criticism
was not muzzled. Administrative action was still held within
bounds by the fact that only specific acts by newspapers or periodicals constituted an offense. [18] The main innovation was the protection of religious groups, which was required by the recurrent
anti-Jewish excesses and anti-Catholic propaganda endangering the
system of religious toleration, one of the cornerstones of the constitutional order.

Numerous newspapers, especially those identified with the
Communist and National-Socialist parties, were suppressed on the
basis of this decree. Yet, sufficient loopholes were left to enable
the radical press to continue its fight against the republic with relative impunity. The press could be silenced, but it could not be
forced to print the truth. Furthermore, the need of the government
for making positive information concerning its policies available to
the public so far had been neglected. The creation of a channel for
positive information was perhaps as important as restrictions,
since the distortion of news by the press was not confined to commission but was frequently achieved through omission. In view of
the general atmosphere of impending doom it was imperative for
the government to make its views known to a public whose sources
of information were normally limited to the party press. The utility of confiscations and suppressions was therefore greatly limited.
To create such a channel of communication between the government
and the people, the government issued another decree in July. [19]
Newspapers and periodicals were now compelled, upon the request
of federal or state governments, to print their declarations or responses to statements without adding or omitting anything, and without making comments or criticising the governmental declaration in
the same issue. Moreover, publications were subject to confiscation or suppression if their contents were likely to endanger public
order and security. The immediate cause for the issuance of the
decree was the conspiracy of silence on the part of a large segment
of the press toward an important radio address by Chancellor

Heinrich Brüning concerning the possibility of a rapprochement
with France. That portion of the oppositional press which chose
to report the address greatly distorted its contents. The government felt that the press had failed to fulfill its obligations toward
the public to the latter's detriment. [20]

The new decree created fears in wide circles that any sem-
blance of freedom of the press was now abolished and that the government henceforth would force its opinions on the press, rather
than accept its guidance. To counteract such fears the federal
ministry of the interior gave assurances to the effect that the sole
purpose of the measure was to restrain the irresponsible party
press, [21] which by this time had few, if any, scruples about dis-
torting the truth in any way that served its political purposes. In
the light of prevailing conditions the justification of the decree can
not be in dispute. Since the party press (Gesinnungspresse) was
more widely read than the commercial press (Geschäftspresse),
readers of the radical press could not be easily acquainted with
the views of the government. The correction of distorted facts
was of particular importance to pacify the excited masses, whose
emotions were being systematically whipped up by the radical parties. The provision that the newspaper affected could not comment
on the governmental declaration in the same issue was more problematical. However, the measure would have been utterly ineffective in the absence of this proviso. Governmental declarations
would then have given the oppositional press an opportunity not only
to rob them of all significance, but also to use them as a spring-
board for especially devastating attacks. Independent thought on the
part of the readers would thereby have been even more discouraged.
That the government should at times have found the temptation to
abuse that privilege hard to resist is small wonder. The government could, for example, issue a statement pertaining to elections
in the last pre-election issue of a newspaper. An undue advantage
would thereby be given to the parties of the governmental coalition.
An illustration of that danger was a declaration of the Prussian state
government against a referendum instigated by the right and the
Communists for the dissolution of the Prussian legislative assembly,
which all Prussian newspapers were compelled to print. [22] In this
declaration the government admonished the voters in view of the imminent regular elections not to participate in the referendum since
the sole purpose of the radical parties was to weaken the constitutional system by creating chaos. [23] This contention was no doubt accurate. Moreover, the referendum (which miscarried) was hardly
the proper means, under a parliamentary system, of deciding whether general elections should be held. Yet, the Prussian constitution
provided for this device of direct democracy, and enough votes for
the referendum had been obtained in the initiative. Political parties
therefore had the constitutional right to elicit as many votes as

possible through persuasion. However, the government itself
should have remained aloof of party competition in the electoral
process. In using its privileged position to interfere it certainly
transgressed its authority. Especially reprehensible was the
timing of the governmental declaration in the last pre-election
issue, which deprived the newspapers of an opportunity for editorial comment before the election. In other words, the government had participated on one side of the party struggle, not on
a basis of equality but on preferential terms through the use of
its privileged powers. Nevertheless, this interference, no matter how great a wrong, was a rare and unusual occurrence and
had little bearing on day-to-day operations. Of far greater menace were the confiscations and suppressions permissible in the
event of a potential threat to public safety and order. A rubber
clause as vague as this could easily be turned into a catchall for
unwelcome criticism. [24] Previously, administrative action had
presupposed specific criteria to justify steps against the press.
While ultimate review by the Supreme Court continued to apply,
it was of little value as a safeguard under these pliable standards.
Moreover, prior to the issuance of the decree, administrative
action against the press had been virtually tantamount to the application of criminal law and thereby held the administrative
agencies concerned to some specific standard and procedure. [25]
The situation was different now that the last barriers to administrative arbitrariness were removed. Suppressions became
purely administrative acts which no longer required justification
in terms of specific offenses. The only remaining criteria were
considerations of an administrative nature, having reference to
nothing but the maintenance of public order and safety. In other
words, even the formal freedom of the press provided for in the
Press Law of 1874 was abandoned, and for the first time the
right to criticize was seriously impaired. [26] Reprehensible
though this extension of administrative jurisdiction may have
been, no practical alternatives are discernible. Decisive action
had become imperative. The political and economic tensions
were approaching the breaking point, and the crisis was unduly
aggravated by sensational and alarming news items disseminated
by the radical press. That journalistic sensationalism might
have had disastrous consequences for an already tense society
cannot with justice be denied. In such a situation it was perhaps
unavoidable to give preference to administrative discretion over
judicial procedure.

Many of the defects of these regulations were soon reme-
died through a new decree induced by pressures brought by the
press and its organizations. [27] The concurrent authority of federal and state governments to compel publication of their declarations was likely to create confusion and might even have

resulted in contradictory declarations in the same matter by different levels of government. Hence, consultation with the federal
minister of the interior prior to requests addressed to the press
was made mandatory, and the declarations were limited to five
hundred words. An important procedural improvement was the
acceleration of judicial review of administrative suppressions.
The most serious objection to the treatment of the press, however, remained unchanged. While the government in principle
was willing to limit administrative discretion under the "public-
order-and-safety" clause, a number of political murders and
attacks on railroads made a relaxation appear inexpedient. Therefore the only qualification introduced was the requirement of
ascertaining, before issuing a suppression order, the possibility
of attaining the desired end through a warning and an official
declaration. In less serious cases a warning would have to suffice if the publisher was willing to make reparation by publishing
a correction. Although the hardships imposed by the July decree
were substantially alleviated, the new decree did not actually re-
move the rather serious infringements upon the freedom of the
press.

The practice soon revealed that even under the new decree
a variety of loopholes remained through which the subversive
press could take refuge. Therefore, a further decree was issued
to close the still-existing gaps. [28] Regulations concerning illegal
publications were tightened and the possibilities for the circumvention of suppression orders eliminated. Confinement in prisons
or penitentiaries was substituted for confinement without the loss
of civic privileges (Festungshaft) for journalistic offenders, since
the conditions of such confinement had been so lenient that they
could hardly be considered an effective punishment. [29] In the case
of seditionist acts committed by the press, plates, lineotypes,
and other equipment used in the production process were made
subject to confiscation and destruction regardless of whether or
not they were the property of the main offender or of a participant
in the offense. The purpose was to discourage printers from ac-
cepting orders for the printing of radical publications, which
might result in the total loss of their working capital. [30]

One of the major difficulties in enforcing press regulations
had been the failure by radical publications to provide information
concerning printer, publisher, authors, and responsible editor
required by the Press Law. Such omission would frequently make
enforcement impossible. Therefore the production, distribution,
or storage, wittingly or by neglect, of such illegal publications
was now subject to mandatory prison sentence. Moreover, failure to report the existence of illegal publications not known to the
government by persons having knowledge of them was made a
punishable offense. It was felt that public security could be

maintained only if the police was able to confiscate such publications before they could be distributed. An especially annoying circumvention of press restrictions had been the substitution to subscribers of a prohibited newspaper of another paper of the same political complexion. [31] The various loopholes occasioned a further tightening of the area of freedom permitted the press. [32] Imprisonment was made mandatory for mere derogatory remarks or libel or slander of persons in public life if the insulting fact was stated in public or designed to make the person affected appear as one unworthy of that confidence which he required for a proper discharge of his public function.

This period signaled the transition from a reasonable degree of freedom of the press to regulations which curtailed that freedom beyond the limits compatible with liberal principles. A definite change was introduced by the decree of July, 1931, which gave the government extensive and ill-defined powers over the press which could no longer be reconciled with the basic requirements of constitutionalism. The reason is to be found in the nature of existing conditions rather than in a conscious illiberality. The necessity for curbing the irresponsibility of the press through such positive steps as governmental declarations was especially apparent in view of the frankly partisan orientation of most newspapers. Less imperative and justifiable were the provisions of the October decree. Confiscation of the equipment of printers unaware of the contents of their product, the duty to inform, and the suppression of substitute newspapers introduced an element of insecurity designed to intimidate the press to an extent no longer reconcilable with the principles of a constitutional state. The violation of these principles was especially dangerous in a period of extended legislative paralysis. Since the importance of the Reichstag as a channel between the government and the public was materially impaired, the press had to assume the mediating function to an increasing degree. The coincidence of legislative disability and suppression of the press did much to prevent the German people from assuming that responsibility without which democracy becomes a hollow absurdity. Yet, if there was any hope whatsoever for saving the constitutional order in face of the disintegration of society and the inability of the Reichstag to form a working majority, extensive administrative discretion was indispensable until more normal conditions were restored. This insoluble dilemma points up clearly the real danger point of contemporary constitutionalism. The Weimar republic did not break down under the armed threats of the early period, which were effectively dealt with by force under executive emergency powers. The real challenge to the constitutional order emanated from the collapse of the social and economic fabric, which, on the one hand, produced a total indifference on the part of the people toward democratic

institutions and, on the other hand, buttressed the autocratic
tendencies of the executive, whose appetite had been whetted
through an extended reliance on decree powers.

A people deeply wounded in its national pride by military
defeat and a harsh peace, deprived of much of its economic substance by the postwar disaster of inflation and now confronted
with the loss of opportunities for employment, was not likely to
maintain the calm detachment of an Oxford debating society in
attempting to alleviate its sufferings. Small wonder that a sizable segment of the population committed their inauspicious future to radical creed movements which had shown themselves
devoid of all inhibitions in dealing with social and political problems. For those who expected salvation from the international
class struggle the Communist party provided a haven, while the
faithful of the Teutonic racial cult looked for inspiration to the
equally radical activists who were parading under the banner of
the National-Socialist party. The strategy pursued by these two
radical movements was dictated by their respective ideological
goals. The former was committed to a schism of society into
two antagonistic classes as well as the destruction of the government as the executive agency of the ruling class. By contrast,
the approach of the latter was far more appealing, since its pre-
sumed goal was the promotion of racial unity, an end to which
even persons of a conservative temper could subscribe. Out of
the battle against extraneous elements and the international and
domestic restrictions of the racial will was to emerge a heightened
unity which appeared to many a most noble and desirable aim.
The difficulty of the government in asserting its authority in a
society thus torn asunder was no doubt aggravated by the lack of
a traditional foundation as well as by its commitment to ideological principles which were incapable of realization.

"Presidial" Cabinets: Papen and Schleicher

The control of the press had become so complete under the
Brüning regime that, short of an outright denunciation of its freedom, a further tightening through legislative action was hardly
imaginable. Consequently, it was in the sphere of enforcement,
rather than legislation, that the differences in the treatment of
the press between the Brüning and the succeeding Papen regime
manifested themselves. While the Brüning regime, with rare exceptions, applied restrictions only against the subversive press,
the Papen regime applied them liberally to the press of the pro-
republican parties as well. [33] The main reason for this difference
is apparent. The Brüning government, however objectionable its
action against the press might have been, was motivated by the

desire to preserve the constitutional order; Franz von Papen's cabinet of barons, on the other hand, did not consider the perpetuation of that order a desirable goal. [34] In view of the economic and political situation which the Papen regime had inherited from its predecessor, a fundamental change in the press regulations was not practicable. The number of unemployed had passed the six million mark; the number of victims killed in the weekly political battles continued to mount; and the National-Socialists openly terrorized Jews and political opponents. Hence, the emergency decree issued by the Papen regime in June, 1932, [35] which terminated the emergency decrees of the Brüning cabinet, did not bring about any significant modifications; it merely summarized the earlier measures in a codified form. The only change was the abolition of unnecessary hardships of the press. The relaxation consisted primarily in the elimination of the rules concerning illegal publications, confiscation of newspapers and equipment, the duty to inform, posters and handbills, and the provisions on defamation. [36] Moreover, the maximum duration of the suppression of newspapers was reduced to four weeks. On the other hand, additional restraints were introduced by waiving the obligation of administrative authorities to attempt a settlement through warnings prior to suppression, and by abolishing the limitation on the length of governmental declarations which newspapers were compelled to publish. In essence, however, the government continued to rely in its press policy on the two basic elements of its precursor: (1) suppression of newspapers and periodicals, and (2) compulsory publication of governmental declarations. [37]

When, in December, the Papen cabinet was succeeded by that of Schleicher, all previous measures against the press were repealed and replaced by far milder regulations. [38] The only remaining offenses warranting suppression were violations of the general criminal laws against sedition and preparation of sedition, treason, and the betrayal of military secrets, or if vital interests of the state were involved, the spreading of untrue or distorted facts. Equally, public vilification or defamation of the president of the Reich, vilification or malicious and intentional derision of the Reich, a Land, the Constitution, colors or flags, or of the armed forces remained punishable offenses. The Protection Law, which was to expire on December 31, was suspended and all other press restrictions abolished.

There is little reason to assume that this liberalization was occasioned by a general relaxation of political tensions. It is true, Kurt von Schleicher's advent to power seemed to mark the bankruptcy of the National-Socialist party. It had suffered its first major setback since 1930 in the general elections of November, 1932. Nevertheless, there was neither a noticeable decrease in

their terroristic activities nor an improvement in governmental
efficiency in maintaining public order. Rather, it appears that
Schleicher entertained hopes of establishing a "presidial" government, which, backed by the sympathies of the broad masses
of the people, relied for its support on the president rather than
on the Reichstag. To gain such sympathies he yielded to the demands of the Reichstag and the trade unions to repeal a substantial part of the measures decreed by the Papen government under the emergency powers of Article 48. That such a relaxation
was ill-timed is evinced by the intensification of political turbulence toward the end of the year.

Treatment of the Press by Agencies of Enforcement

The decrees proclaimed by the Brüning, Papen, and Schleicher regimes cannot alone reflect the true situation of the press.
The actual extent of its freedom was dependent perhaps to a
greater extent on the application of restrictions in concrete situations by judicial and administrative agencies. Again, the task
of appraising judicial and administrative action is a difficult one
because of the rare inclusion of cases involving the press in the
official collection of Supreme Court decisions. Nor are many
such reports to be found in legal journals. [39] The failure to make
such decisions public was in itself detrimental to the freedom of
the press, since it substantially enhanced legal insecurity. In
fact, the uncertainty inherent in administrative action guided
solely by the need for maintaining public order and security made
the measure of legal stability all the more dependent on judicial
decisions. This is true despite the constriction of the courts'
jurisdiction over press delicts. The greatest power over the
press was clearly vested in the administration, which imposed
original restrictions without judicial sanction. [40] The influence of
the courts, though by no means negligible, was only secondary.
However, through frequent support of administrative decisions
they were in a position to encourage administrative agencies to
take a broad view of their authority, while recurrent disagreements would have had the opposite effect.
During the last three cabinets before Hitler's advent to power, suppressions of newspapers were frequent occurrences. Only
in rare instances did the Supreme Court reverse administrative
decisions. The extraordinary acquiescence of the Court in administrative actions elicited varying interpretations. For example, it was taken as an indication of a high degree of administrative self-restraint in dealing with the press. [41] It has also
been opined that the docility of the Court signaled the end of its
utility as a check on administrative encroachments and that the

formality of appeal against administrative decisions was a mere sham. [42] The enormous number of suppressions would seem to lend considerable plausibility to the latter view. There is little evidence to support the assumption that the government, during the persistent crisis, normally exercised an exemplary degree of self-restraint. The ardent support of the administration by the judiciary can be explained more simply and convincingly. By 1930 the republic had definitely acquired a bourgeois and moderately rightist complexion. The danger that the Reichstag might be conquered by a leftist radical majority had been averted both by the Brüning measures and by the numerical growth of counter-revolutionary movements. Moreover, the government was admirably equipped to cope with any irregularities emanating from leftist quarters. The judiciary therefore no longer felt compelled to battle against the administration. The far-reaching coincidence of judicial and administrative views produced certain changes in the treatment of the press. First of all, the press was taken to task far more severely now than had been the case previously under the Protection Law. It was also held criminally liable for offenses which were condoned if committed by individuals. Vilification and derision of the government or its symbols, which had been excused previously, were now the object of judicial discountenance. Subjective criteria, by virtue of which the Court used to shield the press, were now forced to yield to such objective criteria as the impression made on an impartial observer. [43] However, there is little justification for the indignation of as eminent an authority as Max Alsberg over the discriminatory treatment of the press. Its wide distribution as well as its great influence upon the minds of people imposed the duty upon the press to conduct itself more responsibly than individuals. Quite obviously the maintenance of public order required a more inclusive definition of "vilification" and "derision" in the turbulent years of 1930-1932 than during the more stable year of 1929. If the maintenance of law and order became the paramount concern of the government, of necessity subjective standards had to yield to an increasing extent to objective criteria of criminality. A question worthy of more serious exploration is whether the government defined its terms so broadly as to stifle full and pertinent adverse criticism.

A novelty in judicial conduct during the Brüning administration was the severity with which the sanctions were enforced equally against radicals of the left and of the right. [44]

The measures of the Brüning administration against the press were aimed primarily at three objectives: (1) to prevent a spread of the general panic caused by the economic crisis; (2) to combat excesses in the struggle between political opponents; and (3) to counteract growing mutual distrust and animosity between the government and citizens. [45] The measures designed to cope with the first category were directed especially against references of an impending or existing inflation. The memories of the inflation of the early 1920's were still fresh in the minds of the people, and the fear of its recurrence might have seriously threatened social peace. The second category included such items as the glorification of National-Socialist excesses and a derision of the victims. The strategy of the National-Socialist press also included intimidation of political opponents by threatening action once the National-Socialists came to power. Especially effective within this over-all strategy was the attack upon the personal honor of their opponents. An example is the systematic smear campaign against the Berlin chief of police, A.C. Grzesinski, who was referred to as a "Jew-bastard." His divorce case was largely distorted, and he was accused of extramarital relations. Grzesinski instigated approximately one hundred suits for libel and slander, in all of which the defendants were sentenced to nominal fines. [46] Slanderous attacks were directed with equal viciousness against private citizens. For example, a National-Socialist newspaper in Weimar published a list of members of a co-operative society operated by Social Democrats, amply adorned with vilifications in order to harm the business and reputation of the individuals involved. [47] Quite naturally, prohibitions most frequently involved publications that had been critical of the government. The standards applied by the Supreme Court were developed in the light of the objective of alleviating existing tensions and of strengthening governmental authority. So, for example, criticism of the government was punishable if presented in a manner apt to undermine popular confidence in the honesty of the government. Much weight was given to the effect a publication was apt to have on public life. However, suppressions based on the general political complexion of a newspaper were not sustained. Truth was no defense if the manner of presentation was likely to exacerbate the political struggle. In other words, criticism of the government was condoned as long as it had a factual basis and was not designed through distortion, misplaced emphasis, or manner of presentation to incite the emotions of the masses. [48]

It lies in the nature of the matter that the protection of the government against vilification presented the thorniest problem. It is in this area that the temptation to curb the freedom of the press beyond justifiable limits is especially strong. Although in the overwhelming number of instances the press could have effectively performed its function had it adhered to the standards set by the law, suppressions for fairly mild, though not necessarily indispensable, criticisms were quite frequent. A few examples selected at random may serve to convey an impression

of the degree of sensitivity reached by the government under the
impact of protracted political tensions. Newspapers were suppressed for such statements as: ''The government wanted to
lead Germany deeper and deeper into serfdom''; ''The Prussian
government preferred the Communists to all other political parties''; ''Juries have applied to National-Socialists standards different from those applied to others''; ''Prosecutors fail to ex-
plore the causes of an offense — courts apply a dual standard
directed against the National-Socialists — the superiors of a
prosecutor shirk responsibility for action''; ''The chancellor is
incapable of German thinking and patriotic attitude''; ''The minister does not feel German and patriotic.''[49] In marked contrast to the indulgent attitude of the Court toward suppressions
based on vilification of the government was its more exacting
performance in cases involving threats to public order and safety, which were mounting in volume toward the end of 1931. The
Court apparently realized the vulnerability of the press to that
type of action and was aware of the failure of the government to
resist the temptation of making liberal use of its vaguely defined
power. In such cases the rulings of the Court frequently deviated
from those of administrative agencies. The Court affirmed the
principle that the political struggle carried on through the medium of the press was not objectionable as such. It was its conduct with unfair means and the general poisoning of public opinion which, in the opinion of the Court, constituted a substantive
evil which the government was entitled to prevent. However, the
threat to public security would have to be a real one to justify
a suppression. The mere provocation of indignation, even in
wide circles, was not considered adequate reason.[50]

    The encroachments upon the freedom of the press under
the Brüning regime, which frequently transgressed reasonable
limits, can perhaps still be condoned by virtue of their motivation
to preserve the constitution. Yet, from a long-range point of
view these practices had unfortunate effects. It taught Brüning's
successors the methods of circumventing constitutional limitations. The governments of Papen and Schleicher, unlike that of
Brüning, had little if any concern with the maintenance of the
constitution. As a result, restrictions were applied with increasing frequency to the press of the moderate left and the center, their devotion to constitutionalism notwithstanding. By contrast, the National-Socialist press was treated more gently after
Papen's truce with the National-Socialist party.[51] Two examples
of actions by the Papen government against the moderate press
will serve as an illustration.[52] The Social Democratic Vorwärts
had assailed the governmental policy of diverting a portion of the
tax revenue for the subsidizing of the National-Socialist storm
troops in the hope of undermining the National-Socialist

movement by integrating its private militia into the governmental forces. The article in question was written in a militant vein but did not vilify the government. The Prussian minister of the interior refused to carry out the request of the <u>Reich</u> minister of the interior to prohibit the <u>Vorwärts</u>. The Supreme Court found a vilification of the government and upheld the authorities of the <u>Reich</u>. In the other example, the <u>Kolnische Volkszeitung</u> had taken the chancellor, Papen, severely to task for certain statements he had made to representatives of the French press, referring to himself as the first and sole representative of all German national forces. He was also accused of jeopardizing German interests through his public acknowledgment of the reasonableness of German war reparations. Even though the newspaper contended that "this chancellor is a catastrophe," the Prussian minister of the interior refused to comply with the request of suppression by <u>Reich</u> authorities. The Supreme Court again upheld the <u>Reich</u> government in spite of the fact that by virtue of its Centrist affiliation the <u>Kölnische Volkszeitung</u> was most unlikely to reach a segment of the population given to revolutionary action against the republican order.

In general, the interpretations of press regulations by the Supreme Court during the Papen regime were broad and detrimental to the press. Relatively innocuous criticisms were held punishable offenses.[53] These prohibitions frequently involved Social Democratic newspapers.[54] A picture emerges whereby the suppression of newspapers no longer was used to prevent political excesses, but rather to stifle criticism that might embarrass the government. Not even the responsible and state-preserving press was any longer assured the right to criticize without running the risk of suppression. The opposition, whether loyal or disloyal, was muffled, and the last remaining freedoms of the press abolished. The freedom of the press was now restricted to the freedom to conform. Thus, the most vital democratic guarantee had been effectively laid to rest in the German republic.[55]

CHAPTER VI

CONCLUSIONS

The condition of the press in Weimar Germany, which has been described in the preceding pages, presents a discouraging picture. Its experience offers little reassurance concerning the feasibility of institutionally introducing substantive rights in an age when dynamic societies are torn by the disruptive forces produced by industrial capitalism. The need for a more secure foundation than the mere preference of an enlightened intellectual élite was apparent from the very outset. The effectiveness of a liberal constitution presupposes a well-integrated society in which individual loyalties to the commonwealth are stronger than those to lesser collectivities. It presupposes an attitude of toleration, which is incompatible with radicalism of any kind. Its adoption at a time of growing radicalism was therefore a palpable absurdity.

The actual relations between press and government reveal, with only occasional exceptions, neither weakness nor incompetence nor neglect of duty on the part of those entrusted with the conduct of public affairs. During the early period from 1918 to 1923 overt attacks upon the republic prevented the system of toleration anchored in the constitution from taking root. The government would have been remiss in its duties had it permitted the freedom of the press full scope at the risk of jeopardizing social cohesion. Rather, the absurdity of the situation lay in the use of constitutional emergency powers, contrived to provide temporary relief in the event of an acute crisis, for the cure of a congenital disability. However, in all fairness, it has to be admitted that the government had no visible alternatives. The dilemma points up the imprudence of establishing a liberal democracy in a period of social disintegration. When the subtle and clever strategy of the right required a long-term statute for the protection of the republic, the freedom of the press was of necessity rather narrowly circumscribed for an extended period. Little objection could be voiced to the basic aim of the law to hold the press to a more responsible standard of conduct, even by those addicted to liberal principles. However, it was ill-suited to engender in administrative and judicial officers that spirit of toleration without which constitutional guarantees remain pious phrases devoid of practical significance.

After its initial stormy period, the republic entered upon an era of relative political and economic stability which lasted from

1924 to 1930. The tranquility prevailing during those years would no doubt have permitted an experiment in toleration. While violent journalistic attacks even then were kept subject to the sanctions of the Protection Law, the press could have been granted considerable latitude within its context. Such a liberalization was prevented by a nationalistic judiciary, which curtailed more severely than ever before the freedom not only of the Communist, but of the entire republican, press for reasons patently not dictated by a clear and present danger. Thus the only opportunity to practice a measure of toleration was nipped in the bud. It would, however, be amiss to assume that the judiciary was corrupt or acted on the basis of sinister Machiavellian considerations. Nothing could be further removed from truth than to accuse the German judiciary of political cynicism. In fact, the highly legalistic tradition of Germany had a strong hold on bureaucracy and judiciary alike. Consequently, judicial decisions were almost invariably unobjectionable from a formal point of view. Rather, they were tinged with a sincere sympathy for the nationalistic point of view, although the judges themselves were not normally National-Socialists. As a result of the traditional nationalism of the right, all rightist movements were regarded as strongholds of patriotism while leftists or republicans were believed to be enemies of the fatherland. [1] Therefore it was not surprising that all existing loopholes of the law should have been used for the benefit of such ''patriotic'' elements as National-Socialists and Nationalists.

When in the wake of the world economic crisis the foundations of the republic began to shake again, neither the rightist nor leftist opposition any longer attempted open rebellion or violent overthrow of the republic. Instead, efforts to undermine the republic were directed toward the arousal of mass emotionalism, attacks on political opponents, and the formation of private paramilitary organizations by various political parties. [2] The purpose of radical activities was to increase the general feeling of insecurity while their armed organizations were to stand by for the eventual seizure of power. The press played an eminently important role in support of this strategy. It was ideally suited to attract dissatisfied segments of the population, whose electoral support would help the radicals to seize power through ''legal'' means. The circumvention of existing legislation for the protection of the republic by the radical opposition confronted the government with a dilemma: the existing gaps had to be closed; yet this could not be done without encroaching on the liberal principles guaranteed by the constitution. The first definite transgression of the constitutional limits by the government eventually occurred under the Brüning regime after legislative paralysis had practically brought to an end the operation of parliamentary government. [3]

Again, no clear-cut alternatives are discernible. Besides, Brüning's admirable attempts to preserve the constitutional order concealed the dangers inherent in his measures. Such attempts promised little success unless further inroads were made into the freedom of the press. Stubborn insistence on that freedom in face of the mounting threats to the republic would obviously have been sheer folly. There can be little doubt that in time of crisis liberal guarantees tend to undermine liberalism because their formation discourages the necessary differentiation between expression used in the service of reason and expression employed to whip up mass emotionalism. Refusal to deal decisively with forces abusing their rights for the latter end could only spell disaster. The situation was exacerbated after Brüning's dismissal when the Papen regime followed along the path which Brüning had opened up, although for the purpose of undermining, rather than preserving, the constitutional order. Under the guise of averting the "Communist danger," which had little reality at the time, the road was prepared for the triumphant entry of the National-Socialists. Both substance and form of the liberal republic were lost in the pursuit of the Communist phantom, a course demanding a consistent denial of constitutional liberties.

During all three phases of the republic there was little possibility for the practical development of a free press. Nevertheless, to accuse the government of malfeasance or authoritarian aspirations would be amiss. Restrictive measures during the early and the latter phases were inevitable if the republic was to survive. More dubious were the administrative means through which restrictive action against the press was carried out. They included confiscation and destruction of newspaper issues and the materials used for their production, suppression of publications for a limited time, and compulsory publication of governmental declarations. The most frequently used devices, confiscation and suppression, were aimed to discourage violations of the law, rather than to maintain public security. These punitive measures, clearly in the nature of criminal sanctions, were imposed by administrative rather than judicial agencies. To invest administrative agencies with such broad judicial powers was tantamount to conferring upon them authority to destroy the oppositional press. Yet, it is virtually impossible to visualize an alternative to this procedure in view of the absence of a loyal and dependable judiciary. In fact, the transfer from the judiciary to the administration of the enforcement of sanctions against the press was fully vindicated by the increased effectiveness with which the fight against the rightist press was pursued after this shift of authority had taken place. [4] This does not, however, justify the assumption that the bureaucracy was in essential sympathy with the republican government. [5] Rather, the explanation is to be found in the fact

that the key administrative posts in the federal government and
in the governments of many of the Länder were in the hands of
persons loyal to the constitution.

Without denying the inevitability of governmental interference with the press, the methods of confiscation and suppression
are by their very nature reprehensible in that they tend to inflict
irreparable damage upon the press without previous hearing or
court trial. Such postpublication methods actually create greater
legal insecurity than does preventive censorship. Extensive dis-
cretionary powers conferred upon administrative agencies provide temptations difficult to resist. This is evinced by the fact
that the plight of the German press was not primarily occasioned
by the substantive limitations of the decrees and laws for the
protection of the republic, which permitted a tolerable degree of
freedom, but rather by their interpretation and application through
administrative agencies.[6] Quite frequently vindictiveness and
narrow-mindedness, instead of considerations of security, were
the reasons for confiscation and suppression. A more generous
treatment might have substantially alleviated the difficulties of
the press without necessarily increasing political tension.

The eventual collapse of the republic, which the frequent
suspension of constitutional restraints were unable to prevent,
requires explanation inasmuch as it bears upon the problem of
liberties. That it was not the result of constitutional impotence
and the lack of machinery to deal with turbulence, is abundantly
demonstrated by the multiplicity of emergency decrees and the
repeated enactments of Laws for the Protection of the Republic.
The faulty application of sanctions by the government provides
only a partial explanation. The problem of the bureaucracy was
aggravated by the federal structure of the Reich, which left a
considerable measure of autonomy to its component parts. Since,
as a general rule, the federal government exercised its authority
through the agencies of Länder governments,[7] it was impossible
for it to enforce its will in Länder having antirepublican governments. It would be idle to expect that, while administrative and
judicial personnel remained unreconstructed, liberal principles
could have been made effective for purposes other than the benefit of the right. Had the republic followed the Bolshevist practice of replacing the entire administrative and judicial personnel,
it might have substantially enhanced its capacity for survival.

The greater share of the responsibility for the debacle
has to be accredited to the patent impossibility of solving major
social problems through criminal laws. The necessity of occasionally resorting to such laws cannot, of course, be denied.
Every government, constitutional or authoritarian, has the right
of self-defense lest it lose its raison d'être. In realizing that
need, the German republic followed rather closely the pattern

established by its monarchical predecessor. However, it is
doubtful that such measures are capable of dealing with modern
political radicalism. In view of the novel revolutionary strategy
of the right, little relief could be expected from decrees or
legislation contrived to cope with violence against, or preparation for a violent or verbal attack on, the constitutional order.
Nor was the republic essentially strengthened by the prohibition
of disparagements of the republic proper, its representatives,
symbols, or institutions. This method of combating seditionist
attacks upon the existing order may have been tolerably effective
in dealing with revolutions of the nineteenth-century variety.
Hence it is small wonder that virtually all defensive efforts of
the republic had a practical effect only upon the activities of
the Communists, who persisted in their resort to overt, or at
best imperfectly veiled, insurrectionist tactics. By contrast,
the radical movements of the right relied primarily on the ideological conquest of the masses. The result was the deterioration
of parliamentary institutions, which were doomed to impotence by
a lack of popular consensus. Laws, such as were devised by the
German government, tended to serve as a shield for, rather than
as a means of striking down, totalitarian enemies of the constitutional order, who were aiming at the disaffection of the loyalties of the citizens through intimidation and exposure of governmental inability to maintain social cohesion. That difficulty
could hardly be overcome as long as constitutional limitations
prevented any interference with the diffusion of positive totalitarian ideologies. An even more formidable predicament was
produced by the very nature of the modern, democratic party
state, which presupposes a measure of social homogeneity and
integration. Republican Germany was vastly deficient in both
as a result of deep social cleavages and a lack of agreement on
the objects of their loyalties. In fact, the republic could ill
afford to allow political parties even the degree of freedom which
they had enjoyed under the imperial government. Resting on a
genuine popular consensus, the latter was not to any appreciable
degree confronted with a real danger of subversion. The extent
of that consensus is amply illustrated by the reluctance with
which the Social Democratic leaders abandoned the monarchy in
1918. Preservation of monarchical continuity through the medium of a regency would probably have evoked far greater en-
thusiasm than the proclamation of the republic. With the latter's
advent vanished the consensus of the people concerning their
most fundamental institutions. Small wonder that the party struggle no longer revolved around the adjustment of economic or
other secondary interests but brought to the fore deep ideological
cleavages shattering the social fabric proper. Under such circumstances the party system was bound to spell the doom of the

republic. The foundation of the republic was further attenuated by the fact that the tactics of the moderate parties were not sufficiently differentiated from those of the radical parties to permit restrictions of the activities of the latter while leaving the moderates unmolested. The latter too had substituted, to an increasing degree, the activism of the street for rational discussion. [9]

These fundamental predicaments compel the conclusion that legislation for the protection of the republic could at best be of temporary value. Its protracted use for setting aright conditions emanating from the underlying defects of the social basis inevitably produced progressive encroachments on basic rights. Extensive restrictions of the freedom of expression provided a weapon which could be propagandistically exploited by anticonstitutional forces, since the masses of the people were not likely to recognize the subtle distinction between speech employed for the promotion of reason and that designed to suppress it. It ignores the fundamental truth that a sine qua non of social cohesion in any commonwealth is the consensus of the people concerning the fundamental premises of constitutional government. Such a consensus will be inhibited, rather than advanced, by stringent protective legislation. The result for the Weimar republic was nothing short of disastrous. The progressive extension of the area covered by this legislation produced an absolutely staggering number of treason trials, directed more against imaginary than against the real enemies at whom the shaft was chiefly aimed. The eventual suppression of all liberties was a virtual inevitability. Moreover, the almost continuous curtailment of leftist activities led to an overdramatization of the dangers from the left. The resulting fear produced, not only an indifference toward the far more real danger emanating from the right, but a positive receptivity to rightist radicalism. That attitude was aided by a total misconception of the theory and practice of National-Socialism, which was not recognized as a movement worthy of serious concern because of its basic irrationalism. Only few were farsighted enough to realize that its conscious rejection of rationalism was the main drawing card of the party in a time haunted by the specter of economic and political disintegration.

In the last analysis, the political difficulties were attributable to the lack of a genuine community of purpose among the citizens of the republic. Such an environment was not conducive to the realization of comprehensive liberties. The adoption of a liberal system is not accomplished by a volitional constituent or legislative act if unsupported by an organic social development. The authoritarian German tradition, combined with a widespread rejection of the constitutional republic, precluded from the outset any optimistic expectations concerning the feasibility of liberalism.   The change from authoritarianism to liberalism cannot be made overnight.   It is not a constitutional charter, but the liberal spirit of a society, which is the mainstay of human freedoms.   This spirit cannot be decreed ad libidinem.   Perhaps the proposal of Hugo Preuss to establish the democratic republic upon a firm foundation before adopting a system of liberties might have provided a working formula. [10] The republic would have been spared the embarrassment of proclaiming freedoms which it was unable to make effective.   Their premature adoption in a society badly divided on political fundamentals and without stable political structure no doubt constituted the major dilemma of Weimar Germany and was responsible for the failure of its liberal constitution.

SELECTED BIBLIOGRAPHY

I. DOCUMENTARY SOURCES

Der Hitler-Prozess vor dem Volksgericht in München. Zweiter
  Teil. München: Knorr & Hirth G. m. b. H., 1924.

Entscheidungen des preussischen Oberverwaltungsgerichts,
  Vol. LXXVII.

Entscheidungen des Reichsgerichts in Strafsachen, Vols. XXII,
  XXVI, LVII, LIX, LXI, LXII.

Entscheidungen des Reichsgerichts in Zivilsachen, Vols. CVII,
  CXVII.

Reichsamt des Innern — Entwurf der Künftigen Reichsverfassung
  (allgemeiner Teil). Berlin: Reimar Hobbing, 1919.

Reichsgesetzblatt, 1918, 1920, 1921, 1922, 1923, 1924, 1926,
  1927, 1930, 1931, 1932.

Stenographische Berichte, Verfassungsgebende deutsche Natio-
  nalversammlung, 1920.

Stenographische Berichte, Verhandlungen des Reichstags, Vols.
  CCCXXVIII, CCCLV, CCCLVI, CCCLXI, CCCLXXVI,
  CCCLXXXI, CCCLXXXV, CCCXC, CCCXCIII, CDXXIII,
  CDXXV, CDXXVI, CDXXVII, CDXLV.

Strafgesetzbuch.

Strafprozessordnung.

Verfassung des Deutschen Reichs vom 11. August 1919.

Newspapers

Berliner Lokal-Anzeiger, 1920. 1922.

Berliner Tageblatt, 1920, 1921, 1922.

Frankfurter Zeitung, 1922, 1923.

Süddeutsche Arbeiterzeitung, 1925.

Vossische Zeitung, 1926.

II. SOURCES ON THE PRESS AND ITS FREEDOM

Books

Albig, W. Public Opinion. New York and London: McGraw-Hill
    Book Co., Inc., 1939.

Angell, N. The Public Mind — Its Disorders: Its Exploitation.
    New York: E. P. Dutton & Co., Inc , 1927.

Baldwin, L. D. Best Hope of Earth. A Grammar of Democracy.
    Pittsburgh: University of Pittsburgh Press, 1948.

Bauer, Wilhelm. Die öffentliche Meinung in der Weltgeschichte.
    Wildpark-Potsdam: Akademische Verlagsgesellschaft
    Athenaion, 1930.

Bechterew, W. von. Die Bedeutung der Suggestion im sozialen
    Leben. Wiesbaden: Verlag von J. F. Bergmann, 1905.

Bömer, Karl. Bibliographisches Handbuch der Zeitungswissen-
    schaft. Leipzig: Otto Harrassowitz, 1929.

Bonald, L.G.A. De l'Opposition dans le Gouvernement et de
    la Liberté de La Presse. Paris: Librairie d'Adrien Le
    Clerc et Cie., 1827.

Brucker, H. Freedom of Information. New York: The Macmillan
    Co., 1949.

Carlé, W. Weltanschauung und Presse. Leipzig: Verlag C. L.
    Hirschfeld, 1921.

Chafee, Z., Jr. Free Speech in the United States. Cambridge,
    Mass.: Harvard University Press, 1946.

_____, Government and Mass Communications. 2 vols.
    Chicago: University of Chicago Press, 1947.

Childs, H. L. An Introduction to Public Opinion. London: Chap-
    man & Hall, Limited, 1940.

Dewey, John, The Public and Its Problems. New York: Henry Holt & Co., 1927.

Doob, L. W. Public Opinion and Propaganda. New York: Henry Holt & Co., 1948.

Dovifat, E. Auswüchse der Sensationsberichterstattung. Stuttgart: Tageblatt-Buchdruckerei, 1930.

_____, Die Zeitungen. Gotha: Flamberg Verlag, 1925.

Gallup, G., and Rae, S. F. The Pulse of Democracy — The Public-Opinion Poll and How It Works. New York: Simon and Schuster, 1940.

Geiger, Theodor, Die Masse und ihre Aktion; ein Beitrag zur Soziologie der Revolutionen. Stuttgart: Verlag von Ferdinand Enke, 1926.

Goebel, Karl, Totaler Staat und Presse. Diss. Heidelberg, 1936.

Groth, Otto, Die Zeitung. Ein System der Zeitungskunde (Journalistik). 4 vols. Mannheim, Berlin, and Leipzig: J. Bensheimer, 1929.

Hocking, W. E. Freedom of the Press — A Framework of Principle. Chicago: University of Chicago Press, 1947.

Ickes, H. L. Freedom of the Press Today — A Clinical Examination by Twenty-Eight Specialists. New York: Vanguard Press, 1941.

Krumbach, J. H. Grundfragen der Publizistik. Die Wesenselemente des publizistischen Prozesses, seine Mittel und Ergebnisse. Berlin and Leipzig: W. de Gruyter & Co., 1935.

Lasswell, H. D. The Analysis of Political Behavior. An Empirical Approach. New York: Oxford University Press, 1948.

_____, Democracy through Public Opinion. Menasha, Wis.: George Banta Publishing Company, 1941.

LeBon, Gustave, The Crowd — A Study of the Popular Mind. New York: The Macmillan Company, n.d.

Lippmann, W. Public Opinion. New York: Harcourt, Brace and Company, 1922.

_____. The Phantom Public. New York: Harcourt, Brace and Company, 1925.

Lowell, A. L. Public Opinion and Popular Government. New York: Longmans, Green, and Co., 1914.

_____. Public Opinion in War and Peace. Cambridge, Mass.: Harvard University Press, 1926.

Manheim, Ernst. Die Träger der öffentlichen Meinung. Brünn: Rudolf M. Rohrer, 1933.

Mannheim, Hermann. Pressrecht. Berlin: J. Springer Verlag, 1927.

McDougall, W. The Group Mind. New York and London: G. P. Putnam's Sons, 1920.

Menz, Gerhard. Die Zeitschrift. Ihre Entwicklung und ihre Lebensbedingungen. Eine wirtschaftsgeschichtliche Studie. Stuttgart: C. E. Poeschel Verlag, 1928.

Milton, John. Areopagitica. Modern Library edition.

Mirabeau, H. G. R. Sur La Liberté de La Presse, imité de L'Anglois, de Milton. London, 1788.

Palmer, P. A. The Concept of Public Opinion in Political Theory. Diss. Harvard, 1934.

Rogers, Lindsay. The Pollsters. Public Opinion, Politics, and Democratic Leadership. New York: Alfred A. Knopf, 1949.

Ruesch, Arnold. Die Unfreiheit des Willens. Darmstadt: Otto Reichl Verlag, 1925.

Salmon, L. M. The Newspaper and Authority. New York: Oxford University Press, 1923.

Schroeder, Th. Free Speech Bibliography. New York and London: The H. W. Wilson Company, 1922.

Schwedler, W. Das Nachrichtenwesen. Gotha: Flamberg Verlag, 1925.

Shearman, M., and Raynor, O. T. (eds.). The Press Laws of Foreign Countries. London: British Foreign Office, 1926.

Tönnies, F. Die Kritik der öffentlichen Meinung. Berlin: J.
    Springer, 1922.

Traub, Hans. Zeitungswesen und Zeitungslesen. Dessau: Dünn-
    haupt Verlag, 1928.

Articles

Bücher, Karl. "Presse, Parteien und Wirtschaftsverbände,"
    Handbuch der Politik (Berlin-Grunewald: W. Rothschild,
    1922), V, pp. 475-81.

Elchinger, R. "Zur Theorie der Pressfreiheit," Zeitungswissen-
    schaft, (1931), No. 6.

Friedrich, C. J. "Die Problematik der Willensbildung in der äusseren
    Politik," Zeitschrift für Politik, XXII (1932), No. 10.

Heuss, Th. "Die Presse," Teubners Handbuch der Staats-und
    Wirtschaftskunde (Leipzig and Berlin, G. B. Teubner 1926), II.

Jöhlinger, O. "Pressfreiheit und Presspolitik," Handbuch der
    Politik (Berlin-Grunewald: W. Rothschild, 1920), I, pp. 189-96.

Kapp, W. "Die Zeitung als Problem," Zeitungswissenschaft, (1926),
    No. 2.

Muenzner, G. "Öffentliche Meinung und Presse," Sozialwissenschaft-
    liche Abhandlungen (Karlsruhe: Verlag G. Braun, 1928), VI.

Niemeyer, G. "A Reappraisal of the Doctrine of Free Speech,"
    Thought, XXVI (1950), No. 97, pp. 251-274.

Posse, E. "Die Zeitung als Wirklichkeit," Zeitungswissenschaft,
    (1926), No. 3.

"Restrictions on the Freedom of the Press," 16 Harvard Law Re-
    view, p. 55 (1902).

III. SOURCES ON CONSTITUTIONALISM IN GENERAL
AND IN GERMANY

Books

Becker, C. L. New Liberties for Old. New Haven: Yale University
    Press, 1941.

Berlau, A. J. The German Social Democratic Party, 1914-1921.
    New York: Columbia University Press, 1949.

Blachly, F. F., and Oatman, M. E. The Government and Adminis-
    tration of Germany. Baltimore: The Johns Hopkins Press, 1928.

Bryce, James. Modern Democracies. 2 vols. New York: The Mac-
    millan Co., 1921.

De Tocqueville, A. Democracy in America. 2 vols. Henry Reeve
    text as rev. by Francis Bowen, ed. by Phillips Bradley. New
    York: Alfred A. Knopf, 1946.

Dewey, John. German Philosophy and Politics. New York: Henry
    Holt and Company, 1915.

Dicey, A. V. Introduction to the Study of the Law of the Constitution.
    9th ed. London: Macmillan and Co., 1950.

Emerson, Rupert. State and Sovereignty in Modern Germany. New
    Haven: Yale University Press, 1928.

Ewing, A. C. The Individual, The State and World Government. New
    York: The Macmillan Co., 1947.

Friedensburg, F. Die Weimarer Republik. Berlin: Carl Habel
    Verlagsbuchhandlung, 1946.

Friedrich, C. J. Constitutional Government and Democracy. Boston:
    Ginn and Company, 1946.

_____. Inevitable Peace. Cambridge, Mass.: Harvard
    University Press, 1948.

_____. A New Belief in the Common Man. Brattleboro, Vt.:
    1945.

Hallowell, J. H. The Decline of Liberalism as an Ideology with
    particular reference to German politico-legal Thought. Berkeley
    and Los Angeles: University of California Press, 1943.

Halperin, S. W. Germany Tried Democracy. A Political History of
    the Reich from 1918 to 1933. New York: Thomas Y. Crowell
    Co., 1946.

Hensel, Albert. Grundrechte und politische Weltanschauung. Tübingen:
    J. C. B. Mohr [Paul Siebeck], 1931.

Hocking, W. E. The Lasting Elements of Individualism. New Haven:
    Yale University Press, 1937.

_____. Man and the State. New Haven: Yale University
    Press, 1926.

Holcombe, A. N. Human Rights in the Modern World. New York:
    New York University Press, 1948.

Jellinek, G. Allgemeine Staatslehre. 3. Aufl. Berlin: J. Springer,
    1929.

_____. Das System der subjektiven öffentlichen Rechte. 2.
    Aufl. Tübingen: J. C. B. Mohr [Paul Siebeck], 1905.

_____. Die Erklärung der Menschen-und Bürgerrechte.
    Ein Beitrag zur modernen Verfassungsgeschichte. Leipzig:
    Verlag von Duncker & Humblot, 1895.

Klöverkron, F. Die Entstehung der Erklärung der Menschen-und
    Bürgerrechte. Berlin: E. Ehering, 1911.

Laski, H. J. Authority in the Modern State. New Haven: Yale
    University Press, 1927.

_____. Liberty in the Modern State. New York: The Viking
    Press, 1949.

Lieber, Francis. On Civil Government and Self-Government. 3d rev.
    ed. Philadelphia: J. B. Lippincott Company, 1891.

Lippmann, W. An Inquiry into the Principles of the Good Society.
    Boston: Little, Brown & Co., 1937.

Loewenstein, K. Erscheinungsformen der Verfassungsänderung;
    verfassungsrechtsdogmatische Untersuchungen zu Artikel 76 der
    Reichsverfassung. Tübingen: J. C. B. Mohr [Paul Siebeck],
    1931.

Luehr, E. The New German Republic: The Reich in Transition. New
    York: Minton, Balch and Company, 1929.

McIlwain, C. H. Constitutionalism, Ancient and Modern. Ithaca,
    N. Y.: Cornell University Press, 1947.

_____. Constitutionalism and the Changing World. New York:
    The Macmillan Co., 1939.

Mason, A. T. Free Government in the Making. New York: Oxford University Press, 1949.

Meiklejohn, A. Free Speech and Its Relation to Self-Government. New York: Harper & Brothers, 1948.

Mill, J. S. On Liberty. London: Everyman's Library, J. M. Dent & Sons, 1947.

Naumann, F. Demokratie und Kaisertum. Berlin — Schöneberg: Buchverlag der ''Hilfe,'' 1900.

Neumann, F. Behemoth. The Structure and Practice of National Socialism, 1933-1944. New York: Oxford University Press, 1944.

Preuss, Hugo. Deutschlands Republikanische Reichsverfassung. 2. erw. Aufl. Berlin: Verlag Neuer Staat G. m. b. H., 1923.

Quigley, H., and Clark, R. T. Republican Germany — A Political and Economic Study. London: Methuen & Co., Ltd., 1928.

Radbruch, G. Rechtsphilosophie. Leipzig: Verlag von Quelle & Meyer, 1932.

Ritchie, D. G. Natural Rights. A Criticism of some Political and Ethical Conceptions. London: Swan, Sonnenschein & Co., 1895.

Ritter, G. Das Sittliche Problem der Macht. Bern: A. Francke A. G. Verlag, 1948.

Rosenberg, A. A History of the German Republic. London: Methuen & Co., Ltd., 1936.

_____. The Birth of the German Republic 1871-1918. London: Oxford University Press, 1931.

Rossiter, C. L. Constitutional Dictatorship. Princeton: Princeton University Press, 1948.

Salander, G. A. Vom Werden der Menschenrechte. Leipzig: Th. Weicher, 1926.

Scheidemann, Philipp. The Making of New Germany. Translated by J. E. Mitchell. New York: D. Appleton and Company, 1929.

Schmitt, Carl. Verfassungslehre. München and Leipzig: Verlag von Duncker & Humblot, 1928.

Schwertfeger, B. Rätsel um Deutschland, 1933 bis 1945. Heidelberg, C. Winter, 1947.

Smend, R. Verfassung und Verfassungsrecht. München and Leipzig: Verlag von Duncker & Humblot, 1928.

Snyder, L. L. From Bismarck to Hitler, The Background of Modern German Nationalism. Williamsport, Pa.: The Bayard Press, 1935.

Stampfer, F. Die ersten vierzehn Jahre der deutschen Republik. Offenbach a. M.: Bollwerk-Verlag Karl Drott, 1947.

Stier-Somlo, F., and Elster, A. (eds.). Handwörterbuch der Rechtswissenschaft. 4 vols. Berlin and Leipzig: W. de Gruyter Co., 1926.

Wheeler-Bennett, J. W. Wooden Titan: Hindenburg in Twenty Years of German History. New York: William Morrow & Co., 1936.

Wieser, F. Das Gesetz der Macht. Wien: Julius Springer, 1926.

Articles

Bagehot, W. "The Metaphysical Basis of Toleration," Literary Studies (London: Longmans, Green, and Co., 1903), III, 204-25.

Brill, Hermann. "Kämpfe um den Rechtsstaat," Die Justiz, VI (1931), No. 7.

Friedrich, C. J. "Rebuilding the German Constitution," American Political Science Review, XLIII (1949), Nos. 3 and 4, pp. 461-482, 704-720.

_____. "Die Entwicklung des amerikanischen öffentlichen Rechts nach dem Kriege," in Otto Koellreutter (ed.), Jahrbuch des öffentlichen Rechts der Gegenwart, (Tübingen: J. C. B. Mohr [Paul Siebeck], 1932), XX.

Huber, E. R. "Bedeutungswandel der Grundrechte," Archiv des öffentlichen Rechts, XXIII Neue Folge (1933). pp. 1-98.

Latham, E. "The Theory of the Judicial Concept of Freedom of
    Speech, " Journal of Politics, XII (1950), No. 4, pp. 637-651.

Loewenstein, K. "Government and Politics in Germany, " in J. T.
    Shotwell, Governments of Continental Europe (New York:
    The Macmillan Co., 1946). pp. 281-569.

Planitz, H. "Zur Ideengeschichte der Grundrechte, " in H. C.
    Nipperdey, Die Grundrechte und Grundpflichten der Reichs-
    verfassung (Berlin: Reimar Hobbing, 1930), III.

Poetzsch, F. "Vom Staatsleben unter der Weimarer Verfassung, "
    in Otto Koellreutter (ed.), Jahrbuch des öffentlichen Rechts
    der Gegenwart, (Tübingen: J. C. B. Mohr [Paul Siebeck],
    1925), XIII.

Renner, K. "Die Menschenrechte, ihre geschichtliche Rolle und
    ihre zukünftige Geltung, " Zeitschrift für soziales Recht, I
    (1929), No. 4.

Thoma, R. "Grundrechte und Polizeigewalt, " Festgabe zur Feier
    des 50 Jährigen Bestehens des preussischen Oberverwaltungs-
    gerichts (Berlin: Carl Heymanns Verlag, 1925).

Watkins, F. M. "Constitutional Dictatorship, " in C. J. Friedrich
    and E. S. Mason (eds.), Public Policy (Cambridge, Mass. :
    Harvard University Press, 1940), pp. 324-79.

IV. SOURCES ON THE FREEDOM OF THE PRESS
UNDER THE GERMAN REPUBLIC

Books

Anschütz, G. Die Verfassung des Deutschen Reichs vom 11. August
    1919. Ein Kommentar für Wissenschaft und Praxis. 4.
    Bearb. 14. Aufl. Berlin: Georg Stilke, 1933.

Apfel, A. Behind the Scenes of German Justice. Reminiscences of
    a German Barrister 1882-1933. London: John Lane, The
    Bodley Head Ltd., 1935.

Besold, A. Das Recht der freien Meinungsäusserung nach Artikel
    118/I der Reichsverfassung. Diss. Erlangen, 1928.

Brecht, Arnold. Federalism and Regionalism in Germany. The
    Division of Prussia. New York: Oxford University Press, 1945.

Bredt, J. V. Der Geist der Deutschen Reichsverfassung. Berlin: Georg Stilke, 1924.

Buecher, K. Gesammelte Aufsätze zur Zeitungskunde. Tübingen: H. Lapp'sche Buchhandlung, 1926.

Bühler, Ottmar. Die Reichsverfassung vom 11. August 1919. Leipzig and Berlin: B. G. Teubner, 1929.

Busch, R. von. Die Beschlagnahme von Druckschriften under besonderer Berücksichtigung der Presse. Diss. Kiel, 1928-29.

Buschke, Albrecht. Die Grundrechte der Weimarer Verfassung in der Rechtsprechung des Reichsgerichts. Berlin: Georg Stilke, 1930.

Colbatzky, F. H. Die Wahrnehmung berechtigter Interessen bei Beleidigungen durch die Presse im geltenden Gesetz und den Entwürfen. Diss. Erlangen, 1927.

Dittmar, Albrecht. Die Beschränkungen der Pressfreiheit durch die Notverordnungen des Reichspräsidenten. Diss. Erlangen, 1933.

Eberbach, W. Der Geheimnisverrat. Diss. Freiburg i. Ba., 1926.

Everling, F. Fort mit dem Ausnahmegesetz. München: Grossdeutscher Ringverlag, 1923.

Flechtheim, O. K. Die Kommunistische Partei Deutschlands in der Weimarer Republik. Offenbach a. M.: Bollwerk-Verlag Karl Drott, 1948.

Flottrong, W. Grundlagen und Hauptfragen des Journalistenrechts. Diss. Königsberg, 1930.

Freytag-Loringhoven, A. von. Die Weimarer Verfassung in Lehre und Wirklichkeit. München: J. F. Lehmanns, 1924.

Gumbel, E. J. Verräter verfallen der Feme. Opfer, Mörder, Richter. Berlin: Malik-Verlag, 1929.

_____. Verschwörer. Beiträge zur Geschichte und Soziologie der deutschen nationalistischen Geheimbünde seit 1918. Berlin: Malik-Verlag, 1924.

Häntzschel, K. Das deutsche Pressrecht. Berlin: Georg Stilke, 1928.

_____. Die politischen Notverordnungen zum Schutze von Volk und Staat vom 28. Februar 1933. Berlin: Georg Stilke, 1933.

Hager, W. Das Recht der freien Meinungsäusserung mit besonderer
    Berücksichtigung der Presse. Diss. Jena, 1928.

Hubrich, E. Das demokratische Verfassungsrecht des Deutschen
    Reiches. Greifswald: Bruncken & Co., 1921

Hüttig, H. Die politischen Zeitschriften der Nachkriegszeit in Deutsch-
    land. Von der ersten Milderung der Pressezensur bis zum
    Locarno Vertrag. Diss. Leipzig, 1928.

Kiesow, W., and Zweigert, E. Gesetz zum Schutz der Republik nebst
    den Ausführungsverordnungen des Reichs. Mannheim: J.
    Benshelmer, 1923.

Kirchner, J. Die Grundlagen des deutschen Zeitschriftenwesens.
    Leipzig: Karl W. Hiersemann, 1928.

Kitzinger, F. Das Reichsgesetz über die Presse vom 7. Mai 1874.
    Tübingen: J. C. B. Mohr [Paul Siebeck], 1920.

Klein, F. J. Friedensjustiz und Presse. Bonn: 1916.

Lobe, A. Die Gesetzgebung des Reiches und der Länder zum
    Schutze der Republik. Berlin: Otto Liebmann, 1922.

Lobigs, P. Pressenötigung. Diss. Köln, 1939.

Lorenz, Erich. Die Entwicklung des Deutschen Zeitschriftenwesens-
    Eine statistische Untersuchung. Charlottenburg: Rudolf Lorenz
    Verlag, 1937.

Lüddecke, Th. Die Tageszeitung als Mittel der Staatsführung. Ham-
    burg: Hanseatische Verlagsanstalt, 1933.

Mattern, Johannes. Bavaria and the Reich. The Conflict over the
    Law for the Protection of the Republic. Baltimore: The Johns
    Hopkins Press, 1923.

Meissner, G. F. Das Verbot periodischer Druckschriften. Diss.
    Erlangen, 1934.

Meissner, Otto. Das neue Staatsrecht des Reichs und seiner Länder.
    2. Aufl. Berlin: Reimar Hobbing, 1921.

Meissner, Werner. Die Ansichten über die Anonymität in der
    Deutschen Presse vor und nach 1933. Diss. Leipzig, 1936.

Meynen, O., and Reuter, F. Die Deutsche Zeitung. Wesen und
    Wertung. München and Leipzig: Verlag von Duncker & Humb-
    lot, 1928.

Neumann, Franz. Das gesamte Pressenotrecht vom 4. Februar
    1933. Systematischer Kommentar. Berlin: Verlag J. H. W.
    Dietz Nachf. G.m.b.H., 1933.

Nipperdey, H. C. Die Grundrechte und Grundpflichten der Reichs-
    verfassung. 3 vols. Berlin: Reimar Hobbing, 1930.

Poetzsch-Heffter, F. Handkommentar der Reichsverfassung. 3.
    Aufl. Berlin: Verlag von Otto Liebmann, 1928.

Reichspublizistik und Presse. Führer durch die Kollektivausstellung
    der Reichsregierung auf der internationalen Presseausstellung
    Pressa Köln, herausg. vom Reichsministerium des Innern.
    Berlin: Reichsdruckerei, 1928.

Rummel, F. Die rechtliche Freiheit der Presse im liberalen und
    nationalsozialistischen deutschen Staat. Diss. Göttingen,
    1935.

Rumpeltin, E. A. Zeugniszwang gegen die Presse. Diss. Leipzig,
    1931.

Salomon, E. von. Die Geächteten. Berlin: Rowohlt Verlag, 1933.

Scheidemann, K. Die Neutralität des Staates gegenüber der
    Tagespresse. Diss. Handelshochschule, Berlin, 1933.

Schumacher, Karl. Die Redaktionskommission des Verfassungsaus-
    schusses. Berlin: Georg Stilke, 1927.

Watkins, F. M. The Failure of Constitutional Emergency Powers
    under the German Republic. Cambridge, Mass.: Harvard
    University Press, 1939.

Westphalen-Fürstenberg, Ed. Das Problem der Grundrechte im
    Verfassungsleben Europas. Wien: Julius Springer, 1935.

Wettstein, O. Über das Verhältnis zwischen Staat und Presse mit
    besonderer Berücksichtigung der Schweiz. Zurich: Albert
    Müller's Verlag, 1904.

Pamphlets and Articles

Alsberg, M. "Zeitungsverbote," Zeitungswissenschaft (1932), Heft 6, pp. 330-38.

Arian und Oesterle, "Der Begriff der Gefährdung der öffentlichen Sicherheit und Ordnung bei Pressverboten," Die Justiz, V (1932), No. 4.

Bell, "Verschärfung des Ehrenschutzes und Sicherung der verantwortungsbewussten Presse. Strafrechtsreform," Juristische Wochenschrift, LXI (1932).

Brewer, "Zur Freiheit der Pressberichte. Bemerkungen zu dem Potsdamer Prozess gegen von Oppen vom Dezember 1926," Deutsche Richterzeitung, XIX (1927), No. 2.

Conrad, "Ein grundlegendes Urteil des Staatsgerichtshofs zum Schutz der Republik," Deutsche Juristen-Zeitung, XXVIII (1923), Nos. 9 and 10.

_____. "Reichsgesetz vom 7. Mai 1874 über die Presse," in M. Stenglein, Kommentar zu den strafrechtlichen Nebengesetzen des Deutschen Reichs, 5. Aufl. Berlin: Verlag von Otto Liebmann, 1928, I.

_____. "Vorbereitung des Hochverrats durch Verbreitung von Druckschriften. 'Literarischer Hochverrat'?" Deutsche Juristen-Zeitung, XXXII (1927), No. 11, pp. 800-803.

Dohna, A. Graf zu, "Die staatlichen Symbole und der Schutz der Republik," in G. Anschütz and R. Thoma (eds.), Handbuch des Deutschen Staatsrechts (Tübingen: J. C. B. Mohr [Paul Siebeck], 1930), I.

Ebner, A. "Die Landespressgezetze," Deutsche Juristen-Zeitung, XXVIII (1923), Nos. 3 and 4.

_____. "Die neue Pressfreiheit," Deutsche Juristen-Zeitung, XXIV (1919), Nos. 11 and 12.

Elster, L. "Pressgewerbe und Pressrecht," in L. Elster, Adolf Weber, and Friedrich Wieser (eds.), Handwörterbuch der Staatswissenschaften, 4. Aufl. (Jena: F. Fischer, 1925), VI.

Erbe. "Das neue Gesetz zum Schutz der Republik, " Deutsche
    Juristen-Zeitung, XXXV (1930), No. 7.

_____. "Die Rechtsprechung des Staatsgerichtshofs zum
    Schutz der Republik in Verwaltungssachen, " Deutsche
    Juristen-Zeitung, XXVIII (1923), Nos. 3 and 4.

Everling, F. Der amtliche Kampf gegen die Freiheit. Berlin:
    Brunnen-Verlag — Karl Winckler, 1931.

Everth, E. "Die Zeitung im Dienste der Öffentlichkeit, " Archiv
    für Buchgewerbe und Gebrauchsgraphik, LXV (1928), No. 4.

Falck, C. "Pressgesetz, " in M. von Brauchitsch, Verwaltungs-
    gesetze für Preussen, 24. Aufl. (Berlin: Carl Heymanns
    Verlag, 1930), II.

Feder, E. "Aufgaben des Staatsgerichtshofs, " Berliner Tageblatt,
    No. 321, July 22, 1922.

_____. "Der Mord als politisches System, " Berliner
    Tageblatt, No. 403, August 27, 1921.

_____. "Deutsche Volkspartei und Republik, " Berliner
    Tageblatt, No. 414, September 3, 1921.

_____. "Republikanische Notwehr, " Berliner Tageblatt,
    No. 406, August 30, 1921.

_____. "Schutz der Republik oder Krise, " Berliner Tageblatt,
    No. 305, July 22, 1922.

_____. "Verständigungsfriede mit Bayern, " Berliner
    Tageblatt, No. 359, August 13, 1922.

Freymuth, A. "Fechenbach-Feststellungen fur die Geschichte, " Die
    Justiz, II (1927), No. 4, pp. 366-78.

Grau, Richard. "Die Diktaturgewalt des Reichspräsidenten, " in G.
    Anschütz and R. Thoma (eds.), Handbuch des Deutschen
    Staatsrechts (Tübingen: J. C. B. Mohr [Paul Siebeck], 1932),
    II.

Gumbel, E. J. "Landesverrats-Statistik, " Die Justiz, III (1928),
    No. 4.

_____. "Landesverrat im Strafgesetzentwurf, " Die Menschen-
    rechte. Organ der Liga für Menschenrechte, III (1928), Nos. 9 and

Häntzschel, K. "Das Grundrecht der freien Meinungsäusserung und die Schranken der allgemeinen Gesetze der Reichsverfassung," Archiv des öffentlichen Rechts, X Neue Folge (1926).

_____. "Das Recht der freien Meinungsäusserung," in G. Anschütz and R. Thoma (eds.), Handbuch des Deutschen Staatsrechts (Tübingen: J. C. B. Mohr [Paul Siebeck], 1932), II.

_____. "Das Zensurverbot der Reichsverfassung," Juristische Wochenschrift, LIX (1930), No. 27, pp. 2113-16.

_____. "Der Gesetzentwurf zum Schutze des Pressenachrichtenwesens und über die Bildung von Pressesachverständigenkammern," Zeitungswissenschaft, (1932), No. 4.

_____. "Der Verfassungsschutz der Pressfreiheit," Deutsche Juristenzeitung, XXX (1925), No. 24.

_____. "Die Gefahren des fliegenden Gerichtsstandes bei Beschlagnahmen und Einziehungen von Druckschriften," Juristische Wochenschrift, LVIII (1929), No. 17.

_____. "Die neue Pressenotverordnung," Juristische Wochenschrift, LX (1931), No. 30.

_____. "Die Reform des deutschen Pressrechts," Deutsche Juristen-Zeitung, XXXIII (1928), No. 23.

_____. "Freiheit der Berichterstattung," Vossische Zeitung, No. 306, December 23, 1926 (Beilage "Recht und Leben").

_____. "Pressrecht," in F. Stier-Somlo and A. Elster (eds.), Handwörterbuch der Rechtswissenschaft (Berlin and Leipzig: W. de Gruyter Co., 1927), IV.

Heine, W. "Die Buchhändler-und Druckerprozesse vor dem Reichsgericht," Die Justiz, II (1927), No. 4, pp. 350-65.

_____. "Staatsgerichtshof und Reichsgericht über das Hessische Manifest," Die Justiz, VII (1932), No. 4, pp. 154-66.

Heller, H. "Grundrechte und Grundpflichten," Teubners Handbuch der Staats-und Wirtschaftskunde (Leipzig and Berlin: G. B. Teubner, 1927), II.

Hellwig. "Meinungsfreiheit, Zensur," in H. C. Nipperdey, Die
    Grundrechte und Grundpflichten der Reichsverfassung (Berlin:
    Reimar Hobbing, 1930), II.

Herz, Ludwig. "Der Münchener Dolchstossprozess," Die Justiz,
    I (1925-26), No. 3.

Hippel, E. von. "Das richterliche Prüfungsrecht," in G. Anschütz
    and R. Thoma (eds.), Handbuch des Deutschen Staatsrechts
    (Tübingen: J. C. B. Mohr [Paul Siebeck], 1932), II.

Hirschberg, M. "Der Fall Fechenbach," Die Justiz, I (1925-
    26), No. 1, pp. 46-59.

Hoche. "Die neue Phase im Kampf gegen politische Ausschreitungen,"
    Deutsche Juristen-Zeitung, XXXVIII (1933), No. 2.

_____. "Dritte Notverordnung des Reichspräsidenten zur
    Sicherung von Wirtschaft und Finanzen und zur Bekämpfung
    politischer Ausschreitungen," Deutsche Juristen-Zeitung,
    XXXVI (1931), No. 20, pp. 1277-82.

Isaac, Martin. "Entwurf eines Gesetzes zur Ergänzung des Pressge-
    setzes," Die Justiz, VI (1931), No. 7.

Janich. "Zur Beschlagnahme von Druckschriften," Die Polizei,
    XXIV (1927), No. 1

Junck, J. "Das Reichsgericht und die Grundrechte der Reichsver-
    fassung," Deutsche Juristen-Zeitung, XXXIV (1929), 1254-60.

Kantorowicz, H. "Der Landesverrat im deutschen Strafrecht," Die
    Justiz, II (1926), No. 1, pp. 92-102.

Karger. "Wirtschaftsnot und Notgesetzgebung," Deutsche Juristen-
    Zeitung, XXXVI (1931), Nos. 17 and 18.

Karsch, W. "Carl von Ossietzky," Aufbau, Kulturpolitische Monats-
    schrift, I (1945), No. 3, pp. 219-24.

Klimmer. "Verbote periodischer Druckschriften und Uniformverbote.
    Ein kurzer Überblick über die gesetzlichen Bestimmungen und
    die Rechtsprechung des 4. Strafsenats des Reichsgerichts,"
    Leipziger Zeitschrift für Deutsches Recht, XXVI (1932), 137-56,
    201-19, 273-301, 353-61.

Lehmann, R. "Das neue Gesetz zum Schutz der Republik, " Juristische Wochenschrift, LIX (1920), Nos. 16 and 17.

Lilienthal, von. "Zur Einschränkung der Presse-und Versammlungsfreiheit durch die Verordnung des Reichspräsidenten vom 29. August 1921, " Deutsche Juristen-Zeitung, XXVI (1921), Nos. 19 and 20.

Loewenstein, K. "Legislative Control of Political Extremism in European Democracies, " 38 Columbia Law Review (1938), 591-622, 725-774.

Löwenthal. "Der Landesverrat im Strafgesetzentwurt, " Die Justiz, III (1927), No. 2

Meyer, K. "Presserechtliche Fragen, " Leipziger Zeitschrift für Deutsches Recht, XXV (1931), No. 12.

Oborniker, A. "Schutz der Republik, " Die Justiz, I (1926), No. 6, pp. 514-19.

_____. "Zur Hochverratspraxis des Reichsgerichts, " Die Justiz, III (1928), No. 3, pp. 279-84.

Palyi, M. "Deutsche Politische Zeitschriften, " Handbuch der Politik (Berlin-Grunewald: W. Rothschild, 1922), V.

Pich. "Der Haftbefehl gegen Hau und Artikel 118 der Reichsverfassung, " Deutsche Richterzeitung, XVIII (1926), No. 2.

Posse, E. "Pressfreiheit. Bemerkungen zur Reform des Pressrechts, " Zeitschrift für Politik, XVIII (1928), No. 5.

Radbruch, G. "Landesverrat und kein Ende, " Die Justiz, III (1927), No. 4.

_____. "Der Landesverrat im Strafgesetzentwurf, " Die Justiz, III (1927), No. 2, pp. 103-10.

Riesman, D. "Democracy and Defamation: Fair Game and Fair Comment, " 42 Columbia Law Review (1942), 1085-1123.

Rothenbücher, K. "Das Recht der freien Meinungsäusserung, " Veröffentlichungen der Vereinigung der deutschen Staatsrechtslehrer, No. 4 (1928).

Schoenborn, W. ''Die Notverordnungen,'' in G. Anschütz and R.
    Thoma (eds.), Handbuch des Deutschen Staatsrechts (Tübingen:
    J. C. B. Mohr [Paul Siebeck], 1932), II.

Schücking, L. ''Landesverrat und Friedensvertrag,'' Die Justiz, III
    (1928), Nos. 5 and 6, pp. 509-16.

Smend, R. ''Das Recht der freien Meinungsäusserung,'' Veröffent-
    lichungen der Vereinigung der deutschen Staatsrechtslehrer,
    No. 4 (1928).

Spiecker, K. ''Das deutsche Reichspresseamt,'' Zeitungswissen-
    schaft (1926), No. 9.

Thoma, R. ''Das System der subjektiven öffentlichen Rechte und
    Pflichten,'' in G. Anschütz and R. Thoma (eds.), Handbuch des
    Deutschen Staatsrechts (Tübingen: J. C. B. Mohr [Paul Sie-
    beck], 1932), II.

Ule, C. H. ''Über die Auslegung der Grundrechte,'' Archiv des
    öffentlichen Rechts, XXI Neue Folge (1931), pp. 37-123.

Wegner, A. ''Über Hochverrat,'' Die Justiz, III (1927), No. 2.

* * * , ''Calumniare audacter! Neuer Gebrauch eines alten
    Rezeptes,'' Die Justiz, VIII (1932), Nos. 2 and 3.

* * * , ''Das Verbot der 'Kölnischen Volkszeitung' und des
    'Vorwärts,' '' Die Justiz, VII (1932), Nos. 10 and 11, pp.
    482-96.

NOTES

CHAPTER I

[1] Frederick L. Schuman, The Commonwealth of Man (New York: Alfred A. Knopf, 1952), 180.

[2] For an excellent discussion of this theme, see A. Müller-Armack, Das Jahrhundert ohne Gott. Zur Kultursoziologie unserer Zeit (Munster: Regensberg, 1948), chap. xi.

[3] The importance of a free press for modern government was already formulated by H. G. R. Mirabeau, Sur La Liberté de La Presse, imité de L'Anglois, de Milton (London: 1788), 61: "...enlevez, dis-je, à l'Angleterre la liberté de la presse, et malgré toutes les ressources de son admirable constitution, les bévues ministérielles, si rares en Angleterre, s'y succéderont aussi rapidement qu'ailleurs...."

[4] For an elaboration of this theme, see E. Forsthoff, "Zur verfassungsrechtlichen Stellung and inneren Ordnung der Parteien," Deutsche Rechts-Zeitung, 1950, pp. 313 ff.

[5] Admirable discussions of this problem are contained in: C. J. Friedrich, Constitutional Government and Democracy (Boston: Ginn and Company, 1946), chap. xiii; F. M. Watkins, The Failure of Constitutional Emergency Powers under the German Republic (Cambridge, Mass.: Harvard University Press, 1939), passim; and C. L. Rossiter, Constitutional Dictatorship (Princeton: Princeton University Press, 1948), passim.

[6] This survey is based on the monumental work Otto Groth, Die Zeitung. Ein System der Zeitungskunde (Journalistik), 4 vols. (Mannheim, Berlin, and Leipzig: J. Bensheimer, 1928-1930).

CHAPTER II

[1] RGBl, 1918, p. 1303.

[2] Friedrich Stampfer, Die ersten vierzehn Jahre der deutschen Republik (Offenbach a. M.: Bollwerk-Verlag Karl Drott, 1947), 98.

[3] Cf. Ferdinand Tönnies, Die Kritik der öffentlichen Meinung (Berlin: J. Springer, 1922), 126.

[4] The bill of rights of the constitution of 1849 served as a model for that of the Weimar constitution. Cf. K. Loewenstein, "Government and Politics in Germany, " in J. T. Shotwell, Governments of Continental Europe (New York: The Macmillan Co., 1946), 301.

[5] G. Anschütz, Die Verfassung des Deutschen Reichs vom 11. August 1919. Ein Kommentar fur Wissenschaft und Praxis, 4 Bearb., 14. Aufl. (Berlin: Georg Stilke, 1933), 507-508.

[6] K. Häntzschel, "Der Verfassungsschutz der Pressfreiheit, " Deutsche Juristenzeitung, XXX (1925), 1845 ff.

[7] Anschütz, Die Verfassung des Deutschen Reichs, 508-10.

[8] Sten. Ber., CCCXXVIII, 1495.

[9] Hugo Preuss, Deutschlands Republikanische Reichsverfassung, 2. erw. Aufl. (Berlin: Verlag Neuer Staat G. m. b. H., 1923), 89-91.

[10] Häntzschel, "Der Verfassungsschutz der Pressfreiheit, " loc. cit., 1845-48.

[11] K. Häntzschel, "Das Grundrecht der freien Meinungsäusserung und die Schranken der allgemeinen Gesetze der Reichsverfassung, Archiv des öffentlichen Rechts, X N. F. (1926), 236.

[12] Karl Schumacher, Die Redaktionskommission des Verfassungsausschusses (Berlin: Georg Stilke, 1927), 60-61.

[13] Entscheidungen des preussischen Oberverwaltungsgerichts, LXXVII, 519.

[14] Cf. K. Rothenbücher, "Das Recht der freien Meinungsäusserung, " Veröffentlichungen der Vereinigung der deutschen Staatsrechtslehrer, No. 4 (1928), 19-20. This view was supported by the Federal Supreme Court, as quoted in Juristische Wochenschrift, LIX (1930), 268-69.

[15] Häntzschel, "Das Grundrecht der freien Meinungsäusserung und die Schranken der allgemeinen Gesetze der Reichsverfassung, " loc. cit., 232-33.

16 Cf. J. V. Bredt, Der Geist der Deutschen Reichsverfassung
(Berlin: Georg Stilke, 1924), 270.

17 Cf. Note 14, supra.

18 Cf. F. Poetzsch-Heffter, Handkommentar der Reichsverfassung, 3. Aufl. (Berlin: Verlag von Otto Liebmann, 1928),
417: "Bei der Abwängung der verschiedenen Interessen hat
der Gesetzgeber Ermessensspielraum. Er hat aber bei
Erlass des einzelnen Gesetzes die in der Rechtsordnung zum
Ausdruck kommenden Massstäbe anzuwenden und kann von
ihnen ausnahmsweise nur abweichen, wenn ein dringendes
Interesse des Gemeinwohls hierzu beim Vorliegen neuer und
besonderer Umstände zwingt. "

19 Cf. O. Jöhlinger, "Pressfreiheit und Presspolitik, " Handbuch
der Politik (Berlin-Grunewald: W. Rothschild, 1920), I, 190.

20 Cf. Anschütz, Die Verfassung des Deutschen Reichs, 558;
Poetzsch-Heffter, Handkommentar der Reichsverfassung,
420; K. Häntzschel,"Das Zensurverbot der Reichsverfassung,"
Juristische Wochenschrift, LIX (1930), 2113-16.

21 Gewerbeordnung, Section 56, para. 4, and Section 42a.

22 Examples of court decisions supporting the continued applica-
bility of previous police control are the following:
Entscheidungen des Bayerischen Verwaltungsgerichtshofs,
XLIII, 21; Entscheidungen des Reichsgerichts in Strafsachen,
LIX, 158 ff.; Preussisches Oberverwaltungsgericht, decision
of December 9, 1926, cited by Häntzschel, "Das Zensurverbot
der Reichsverfassung," loc. cit., 2113-16.

23 Preuss, Deutschlands Republikanische Reichsverfassung, 95.

24 The topic is discussed by R. Thoma in H. C. Nipperdey, Die
Grundrechte und Grundpflichten der Reichsverfassung (Ber-
lin: Reimar Hobbing, 1930), II, 4; also see R. Thoma,
"Grundrechte und Polizeigewalt, " Festgabe zur Feier des
50jährigen Bestehens des preussischen Oberverwaltungs-
gerichts (Berlin: Carl Heymanns Verlag, 1925), and "Das
System der subjektiven öffentlichen Rechte und Pflichten, "
in G. Anschütz and R. Thoma (eds.), Handbuch des Deutschen
Staatsrechts (Tübingen: J. C. B. Mohr [Paul Siebeck], 1932),
II, 607 ff.; G. Jellinek, Allgemeine Staatslehre, 3. Aufl.
(Berlin: J. Springer, 1929), 419-21; Albert Hensel,

Grundrechte und politische Weltanschauung (Tübingen: J. C.
B. Mohr [Paul Siebeck], 1931), 9-10, C.H. Ule, "Über die
Auslegung der Grundrechte, " Archiv des öffentlichen
Rechts, XXI N.F. (1931), 37-123.

25   Cf. J.H. Hallowell, The Decline of Liberalism as an Ideology
with Particular Reference to German Politico-Legal Thought
(Berkeley and Los Angeles: University of California Press,
1943), passim. The position of the German Supreme Court
was ambiguous. There are decisions supporting the natural-
law point of view (Entscheidungen des Reichsgerichts in
Strafsachen, LXII, 65 ff.; Entscheidungen des Reichsgerichts
in Zivilsachen, CXXV, 422), as well as reinforcements of the
positivist view (Entscheidungen des Reichsgerichts in
Zivilsachen, CXVIII, 327, and CII, 161.)

26   Views similar to the American practice of judicial review were
voiced by H. Triepel, as cited by Thoma in Nipperdey, Die
Grundrechte und Grundpflichten der Reichsverfassung, II,
22-23.

27   C. J. Friedrich, "Rebuilding the German Constitution, "
American Political Science Review, XLIII (1949), 463.

28   Cf. E.R. Huber, "Bedeutungswandel der Grundrechte, "
Archiv des öffentlichen Rechts, XXIII N.F. (1933), 16; K.
Renner, "Die Menschenrechte, ihre geschichtliche Rolle
und ihre zukünftige Geltung, " Zeitschrift für soziales Recht,
I (1929), 230-33.

29   See pp. 5-7.

30   Richard Grau, "Die Diktaturgewalt des Reichspräsidenten, " in
Anschütz and Thoma (eds.), Handbuch des Deutschen Staatsrechts, II, 294.

31   Reichspressgesetz vom 7. Mai 1874, RGBl, p. 65, as amended,
RGBl, 1883, p. 163.

32   Cf. Otto Meissner, Das neue Staatsrechts des Reichs und seiner
Länder, 2 Aufl. (Berlin: Reimar Hobbing, 1921), 235.

33   L. Elster, "Pressgewerbe und Pressrecht, " in L. Elster,
Adolf Weber, and Friedrich Wieser (eds.), Handwörterbuch
der Staatswissenschaften (Jena: F.Fischer, 1925), VI, 1080.

34   Allgemeines Landrecht, section 10 II 17.

35 C. Falck, "Pressgesetz, " in M. von Brauchitsch, Verwaltungs-
    gesetze für Preussen, 24. Aufl. (Berlin: Carl Heymanns
    Verlag, 1930), II, 270-71.

36 Hermann Mannheim, Pressrecht (Berlin: J. Springer Verlag,
    1927), 21.

37 This was not a unique feature of the German Press Law. Simi-
    lar provisions could be found in the French Law on the Free-
    dom of the Press of July 29, 1881, as cited by M. Shearman
    and O. T. Raynor, The Press Laws of Foreign Countries
    (London: British Foreign Office, 1926), 90-103.

38 Entscheidungen des Reichsgerichts in Strafsachen, XXXII, 220-
    23, as cited by Mannheim, Pressrecht, 75.

39 K. Hantzschel, "Die Gefahren des fliegenden Gerichtsstandes
    bei Beschlagnahme und Einziehung von Druckschriften, "
    Juristische Wochenschrift, LVIII (1929), 1178-79.

40 Confiscation served several purposes: (1) the securing of evi-
    dence; (2) the safeguarding of objects which were likely to be
    seized by the courts; (3) the enforcement of press regulations
    contained in the Press Law; (4) the prevention of danger to
    public safety and order in the event of an external or internal
    crisis. Cf. Elster "Pressgewerbe und Pressrecht, " in Elster,
    Weber, and Wieser (eds.), Handwörterbuch der Staatswissen-
    schaften, VI, 1084-85; F. Kiztinger, Das Reichsgesetz über
    die Presse vom 7. Mai 1874 (Tübingen: J. C. B. Mohr [Paul
    Siebeck], 1920), 175; R. von Busch, Die Beschlagnahme von
    Druckschriften unter besonderer Berücksichtigung der
    Presse (Diss. Kiel, 1928-29), 30.

41 Falck, "Pressgesetz, " in Brauchitsch, Verwaltungsgesetze für
    Preussen, II, 300-303.

42 Cf. A. Ebner, "Die Landespressgesetze, " Deutsche Juristen-
    zeitung, XXVIII (1923), 104.

43 K. Häntzschel, "Pressrecht, " in F. Stier-Somlo and A. Elster
    (eds.), Handwörterbuch der Rechtswissenschaft (Berlin and
    Leipzig: W. de Gruyter Co., 1927), IV, 557.

44 E. Everth, "Die Zeitung im Dienste der Öffentlichkeit, " Archiv
    für Buchgewerbe und Gebrauchsgraphik, LXV (1928), No. 4,
    p. 29.

[45] Cf. F.H. Colbatzky, Wahrnehmung berechtigter Interessen bei Beleidigung durch die Presse im geltenden Gesetz und den Entwürfen (Diss. Erlangen, 1927), passim; O. Meynen and F. Reuter, Die Deutsche Zeitung. Wesen und Wertung (München and Leipzig: Verlag von Duncker & Humblot, 1928), 108; E.A. Rumpeltin, Zeugniszwang gegen die Presse (Diss. Leipzig, 1931), 21.

[46] Cf. Entscheidungen des Reichsgerichts in Strafsachen, XXVI, 76, and LVI, 380; decision Oberlandesgericht, Jena, March 26, 1926, cited in Juristische Wochenschrift, LV (1926), 2225.

[47] Bayerisches Oberlandesgericht, XXVI, 71.

[48] Entscheidungen des Reichsgerichts in Zivilsachen, V, 240; Entscheidungen des Reichsgerichts in Strafsachen, LVI, 382.

[49] K. Häntzschel, Das deutsche Pressrecht (Berlin: Georg Stilke, 1928), 8-9.

[50] Ibid., 24-25.

CHAPTER III

[1] A. Rosenberg, A History of the German Republic (London: Methuen & Co., Ltd., 1936), chap. 1, passim.

[2] O.K. Flechtheim, Die Kommunistische Partei Deutschlands in der Weimarer Republik (Offenbach a. M.: Bollwerk-Verlag Karl Drott, 1948), 42.

[3] Rosenberg, History of the German Republic, 63.

[4] Ibid., chap. ii, passim.

[5] Stampfer, Die ersten vierzehn Jahre der deutschen Republik, 91.

[6] The history of the Free Corps movement and their eventual transition into the Nazi party is excellently and reliably presented by R.G.L. Waite, Vanguard of Nazism. The Free Corps Movement in Postwar Germany, 1918-1923 (Cambridge, Mass.: Harvard University Press, 1952).

[7] Cf. Stampfer, Die ersten vierzehn Jahre der deutschen Republik, 92. Crimes of this nature included the murder of the Sparta-cist leaders Karl Liebknecht and Rosa Luxemburg.

[8] Flechtheim, Die Kommunistische Partei Deutschlands in der Weimarer Republik, 51-2.

[9] Jöhlinger, "Pressfreiheit und Presspolitik, " Handbuch der Politik, I, 195.

[10] Flechtheim, Die Kommunistische Partei Deutschlands in der Weimarer Republik, 52.

[11] F. Friedensburg, Die Weimarer Republik (Berlin: Carl Habel Verlagsbuchhandlung, 1946), 167.

[12] Berliner Tageblatt, No. 14, January 8, 1920.

[13] Verordnung des Reichspräsidenten zur Wiederherstellung der öffentlichen Sicherheit und Ordnung vom 11. und 13. Januar 1920, RGBl I, 207 ff.

[14] Berliner Tageblatt, No. 36, January 20, 1920, reports that fifteen papers of the USPD and KPD were being suppressed until further notice.

[15] Berliner Lokal-Anzeiger, No. 25, January 14, 1920.

[16] Ibid.

[17] Berliner Tageblatt, No. 35, January 20, 1920.

[18] Ibid.

[19] Berliner Tageblatt, No. 37, January 21, 1920.

[20] This was the upper chamber of the legislature composed and operating on the basis of the federal principle.

[21] For an excellent discussion of this strategy see D. Riesman, "Democracy and Defamation: Fair Game and Fair Comment, " 42 Columbia Law Review (1942), 1085-1123.

[22] Early in January the Deutsche Zeitung wrote: "Aus der Hand der von ihm missleiteten Masse empfängt der Demagoge seine Strafe.... Der Krug geht nur solange zum Brunnen, bis er bricht. Und weiter wird gesagt, dass auf der Stirne Erzbergers der Makel der Leute brenne, die dem Heere mit dem Dolche in den Rücken gefallen seien. " Further examples of press agitation connected with this incident can be found in Berliner Tageblatt, No. 49, January 27, 1920.

23
Cf. Demokratische Korrespondenz, as cited in Berliner Tageblatt, No. 54, January 30, 1920.

24
Cf. address by the Prussian minister of the interior, Wolfgang
Heine, to the 107th session of the Prussian Landesversamm-
lung, as quoted by the Berliner Tageblatt, No. 54, January
30, 1920.

25
Berliner Lokal-Anzeiger, No. 133, March 12, 1920.

26
Berliner Tageblatt, No. 133, March 12, 1920.

27
Ibid.

28
Berliner Tageblatt, No. 32, January 18, 1920.

29
Cf. Rosenberg, History of the German Republic, 135; Stampfer,
Die ersten vierzehn Jahre der deutschen Republik, 165;
Flechtheim, Die Kommunistische Partei Deutschlands in der
Weimarer Republik, 62.

30
Berliner Lokal-Anzeiger, No. 206, May 4, 1920.

31
Ibid., No. 208, May 5, 1920.

32
Ibid.

33
Berliner Lokal-Anzeiger, No. 221, May 12, 1920.

34
A full discussion of the Communist insurrection of 1920 is contained in Watkins, Failure of Constitutional Emergency Powers,
chap. iii, passim.

35
Ibid., 28-30.

36
Ibid., 31.

37
As a representative example, the Verordnung des Reichspräsidenten auf Grund von Art. 48 Abs. 2 der Reichsverfassung,
betreffend die zur Wiederherstellung der öffentlichen Sicherheit
und Ordnung fur den Bezirk des Wehrkreises I nötigen Massnahmen, vom 23. Juli 1920, RGBl II, 1477, has been used as a
model for this discussion.

38
Both Ebert and Erzberger brought several suits against news-
papers, and so did the Prussian Minister-President Otto
Braun. Berliner Tageblatt, No. 392, August 21, 1921.

39 Cf. Riesman, "Democracy and Defamation...," loc. cit.,
   passim.

40 Berliner Tageblatt, No. 404, August 28, 1921, quotes the nationalist Arnswalder Anzeiger as follows: "Wir wollen nicht
   heucheln. Die Nachricht von dem Mordanschlag auf Erzberger wird bei vielen, die diesen Mann glühend hassen,
   wenn nicht ein frohes, so doch ein erwartungsvolles Auf-
   horchen ausgelöst haben: ist er tot? Und eine unbedenklich
   eingestandene Enttäuschung .... "

41 E. Dombrowski, "Die Schuldigen," Berliner Tageblatt, No. 402,
   August 27, 1921.

42 E. Feder, "Der Mord als politisches System," Berliner Tageblatt, No. 403, August 27, 1921.

43 Verordnung des Reichsprasidenten vom 30. August 1921, RGBl
   II, 1239.

44 For example, see Berliner Tageblatt, No. 410, September 1,
   1921.

45 Cf. E. Feder, "Republikanische Notwehr," Berliner Tageblatt,
   No. 406, August 30, 1921.

46 Berliner Tageblatt, No. 411, September 1, 1921.

47 Ibid., No. 437, September 16, 1921.

48 Entscheidungen des Reichsgerichts in Zivilsachen, CVII, 118 ff.

49 Quoted in Berliner Tageblatt, No. 411, September 1, 1921.

50 Some of the major Communist papers suppressed were: Tribüne in Halle; Der Klassenkampf in Halle; Der Kommunist
   in Frankfurt; Rote Fahne in Berlin; Gothaer Volksblatt, as
   quoted in Berliner Tageblatt, No. 417, September 5, 1921;
   No. 434, September 15, 1921; No. 426, September 10, 1921.

51 Cf. interview of the minister of the interior, Dr. Gradnauer,
   with reporters of the Berliner Tageblatt. Berliner Tageblatt,
   No. 413, September 2, 1921.

52 Ibid., No. 417, September 5, 1921.

53 Ibid., No. 411, September 1, 1921.

54 Ibid., No. 426, September 10, 1921.

55 Bezirksverband Berlin im Reichsverband der Deutschen Presse,
    quoted ibid., No. 414, September 3, 1921.

56 Vereinigung grosstädtischer Zeitungsverleger, quoted ibid., No.
    416, September 4, 1921.

57 Verein deutscher Zeitungsverleger, quoted ibid., No. 418.

58 This view is borne out by an opinion of the Court of State for the
    protection of the republic, which was established the following
    year subsequent to the assassination of Rathenau: "Offensicht-
    lich handelt es sich hier nicht darum, unmittelbar, durch eine
    vollständige oder lange dauernde Einstellung der Denkschrift
    die in ihr zutage getretene staatsgefährdende Gesinnung
    unschadlich zu machen, sondern es sollte wegen einer vorge-
    kommenen Verfehlung Verlag und Schriftleitung durch ein Übel
    getroffen und damit mittelbar ferneren Verfehlungen vorge-
    beugt werden." Beschluss vom 19. September 1922 (St. R. 18.
    248), quoted in Sten. Ber., Drucksache, CCCLXXVI, No.
    5444, p. 5917.

59 Riesman, "Democracy and Defamation...," loc. cit., 1092.

60 The Kreuzzeitung, for example, reporting an address by Gen-
    eral von Deimling stating that reconstruction was possible
    only within the context of the democratic republic, remarked:
    "Wir schämen uns dieses Generals." Quoted in Berliner
    Tageblatt, No. 257, June 2, 1922.

61 Stampfer, Die ersten vierzehn Jahre der Deutschen Republik,
    274-75, maintains that there was no objective basis for the
    strong animosity of the right against Scheidemann in view of
    his poverty and sincere patriotism. Stampfer concedes that
    a socialist of as much patriotic sentiment as Scheidemann
    was perhaps especially resented by the nationalists. Mani-
    festly, failure to challenge the integrity of such a man would
    have detracted from the effectiveness of the rightist propa-
    ganda campaign, which was based primarily on the alleged
    antinationalism of the socialists.

62 Stampfer, ibid., 275.

63 Cf. Rosenberg, History of the German Republic, 160.

64 Berliner Tageblatt, No. 289, June 22, 1922; ibid., No. 293, June
    24, 1922.

65 Sten. Ber., CCCLV, 8034. Also see E. von Salomon, Die
Geächteten (Berlin: Rowohlt Verlag, 1923).

66 Sten. Ber., CCCLV, 8037.

67 Verordnung des Reichspräsidenten zum Schutz der Republik vom
26. Juni 1922, RGBl, 521 ff.

68 The second decree for the protection of the republic of June 29,
1922, RGBl, 532, extended the sanctions to "whoever de-
fames or vilifies in public the deceased victims of such acts
of violence."

69 Sten. Ber., CCCLVI, 8044-72.

70 Crispien of the USPD, ibid., 8052. The same desire was expressed by Koenen of the KPD, ibid., 8065.

71 Ibid., 8050.

72 Ibid., 8046.

73 Representative Hergt of the Nationalist party, Sten. Ber.,
CCCLVI, 8049-50.

74 Representative Heinze of the People's party, ibid., 8058-59.

75 Koenen, ibid., 8065; Crispien, ibid., 8053.

76 Hergt, ibid., 8049-50; Heinze, ibid., 8061.

77 Crispien, ibid., 8053.

78 Berliner Tageblatt, No. 303, June 30, 1922.

79 Cf. Flechtheim, Die Kommunistische Partei Deutschlands in der
Weimarer Republik, 82; Stampfer, Die ersten vierzehn Jahre
der deutschen Republik, 286-88.

80 Any fears that the Communists might overthrow the republic once
the extreme right was liquidated seemed unwarranted. Undoubtedly, many potentially moderate elements, now attracted by the
extreme rightist movements, would have supported the republic
against a Communist threat. It is unlikely that more than a
small fraction would have switched from rightist to leftist
radicalism.

81 For example, many of the nationalist veterans' organizations
    were dissolved in Prussia. Berliner Tageblatt, No. 307,
    July 14, 1922.

82 The Neue Zeitung and the München-Augsburger Zeitung were
    both suppressed for this reason for three days. Berliner
    Tageblatt, No. 308, July 14, 1922.

83 Stampfer, Die ersten vierzehn Jahre der deutschen Republik, 288.

84 Gesetz zum Schutz der Republik, RGBl, 585.

85 Cf. Dr. Adolf Köster, minister of the interior, Sten. Ber.,
    CCCLVI, 8288.

86 Democratic representative Dr. Schücking, ibid., 8430.

87 Dr. Gustav Stresemann, ibid., 8709.

88 Sten. Ber., CCCLVI, 8304, 8488.

89 Representative Graaf (Thuringia), ibid., 8414-15.

90 Editorial by Theodor Wolff in Berliner Tageblatt, No. 336, July
    31, 1922.

91 Riesman points out correctly that the German judiciary was
    neither corrupt nor identified with the Nazi movement, and
    had a profound respect for legalism. However, it was sym-
    pathetic to the aims and ideology of the extreme right. It is,
    therefore, not surprising that they should have used their dis-
    cretion to the advantage of the right. "Democracy and Defa-
    mation...," loc. cit., 1092-93.

92 Berliner Tageblatt, No. 333, July 29, 1922.

93 Verordnung zum Schutz der Verfassung der Republik vom 24.
    Juli 1922, cited by A. Lobe, Die Gesetzgebung des Reiches und
    der Länder zum Schutze der Republik (Berlin: Otto Liebmann,
    1922), 97-99.

94 Cf. Stampfer, Die ersten vierzehn Jahre der deutschen Republik,
    290.

95 A declaration was issued by the government of the Reich expound-
    ing the unconstitutionality of the Bavarian decree. Berliner
    Tageblatt, No. 331, July 28, 1922.

96 W. Kiesow and E. Zweigert, Gesetz zum Schutz der Republik
    nebst den Ausführungsverordnungen des Reichs (Mannheim:
    J. Bensheimer, 1923), pp. XXVII-XXIX. Reichsexekutive had
    been invoked repeatedly in the early years of the republic
    against the leftist governments of Central Germany. In the
    case of Bavaria such a step would have been risky because of
    the questionable willingness of the army to proceed against
    antirepublican forces of the right.

97 Berliner Tageblatt, No. 358, August 12, 1922.

98 Ibid.; also Kiesow and Zweigert, Gesetz zum Schutz der Re-
    publik..., pp. XXVII-XXIX.

99 Cf. Sten. Ber., CCCLVI, 8291, 8304.

100 Koenen, ibid., 8714.

101 Cf. Frankfurter Zeitung, No. 620, September 2, 1922.

102 Cf. Berliner Tageblatt, No. 339, August 2, 1922; No. 342,
    August 3, 1922; Nos. 367 and 368, August 18, 1922.

103 Frankfurter Zeitung, No. 619, September 2, 1922.

104 Ibid., No. 620, September 2, 1922.

105 Ibid.

106 "Denkschrift des Ministers des Innern über die Rechtssprechung
    des Staatsgerichtshofs zum Schutz der Republik in Verwaltungs-
    sachen vom 21. November 1922," Sten. Ber., Drucksache,
    CCCLXXVI, No. 5444. This compilation includes predominant-
    ly cases dealing with offenses of the right.

107 Decision of December 6, 1922 (98/22), cited in Juristische
    Wochenschrift, LII (1923), No. 11, p. 517.

108 Cf. Erbe, "Die Rechtsprechung des Staatsgerichtshofs zum
    Schutz der Republik in Verwaltungssachen," Deutsche Juristen-
    Zeitung, XXVIII (1923), Nos. 3 and 4, pp. 81-3.

109 Decision of October 13, 1922 (St. R. V 66/22), cited in Sten. Ber.,
    Drucksache, CCCLXXVI, No. 5444, p. 5917.

110 Decision of September 19, 1922 (St. R. 18.248), cited ibid., 5918.

111 Decision of October 25, 1922 (St. R. 299/22), cited ibid., 5918.

112 Decision of October 25, 1922 (St. R. V 78/22), cited ibid., 5919.

113 Decision of October 27, 1922 (St. R. V 82/22), cited ibid., 5919.

114 Decision of September 19, 1922 (St. R. 305), cited ibid., 5920.

115 Decision of October 25, 1922 (St. G. V 80/22), cited ibid.

116 Decision of September 19, 1922 (St. R. V 6/22), cited in Juristische Wochenschrift, LII (1923), 19-20.

117 Decision of September 19, 1922 (St. R. V 21/22), cited in Sten. Ber., Drucksache, CCCLXXVI, No. 5444, p. 5920.

118 Decision of September 20, 1922 (St. R. 275), cited ibid.

119 Frankfurter Zeitung, No. 669, September 21, 1922, for example, reported that the Court of State had lifted prohibitions issued against the Rote Fahne, Westfälische Arbeiterzeitung, Gelsenkirchener Arbeiterzeitung, and Rote Tribüne.

120 For example, Representative Emminger of the Bavarian People's party referred to the bill in the Reichstag as a Wahlmaulkorbgesetz, Sten. Ber., CCCLVI, 8442. F. Everling in Fort mit dem Ausnahmegesetz (Munchen: Grossdeutscher Ringverlag, 1923), 24, maintained that the law outlawed political propaganda and that silence alone was now legal. Rothenbücher, "Das Recht der freien Meinungsäusserung," loc. cit., 23, objected to the inclusion among criminal offenses of approval or glorification of a political murder, since this meant that the mere expression of an opinion was prohibited. A. Graf zu Dohna, "Die staatlichen Symbole und der Schutz der Republik," in Anschütz and Thoma (eds.), Handbuch des Deutschen Staatsrechts, I, 204, objected that the law was not compatible with the requirements of a constitutional state.

121 Cf. Theodor Wolff in Berliner Tageblatt, No. 324, July 24, 1922.

122 A brief discussion of the case is contained in Stampfer, Die ersten vierzehn Jahre der deutschen Republik, 292-93. A full discussion is provided by Max Hirschberg, "Der Fall Fechenbach," Die Justiz, I (1925-26), No. 1, pp. 46-59; and by A. Freymuth, "Fechenbach-Feststellungen für die Geschichte," Die Justiz, II (1927), No. 4, pp. 366-78.

123 A subcommittee of the committee on foreign affairs of the
Reichstag, set up to investigate the Fechenbach case, stated:
"Dass die Veröffentlichung des sogenannten Ritter-Tele-
gramms auf die Lage des Deutschen Reichs bei den Friedens-
verhandlungen Einfluss geübt hat, ist nicht klargestellt; weder
die Friedensdelegation in Versailles noch das Auswärtige Amt
in Berlin haben dieser Veröffentlichung Beachtung geschenkt. "
Cited by Hirschberg, "Der Fall Fechenbach, " loc. cit. , 58.

124 Cf. Stampfer, Die ersten vierzehn Jahre der deutschen Republik, 292.

125 In its issue of October 26, 1922, it labeled the decision a gross
miscarriage of justice.

126 October 26, 1922.

127 Frankfurter Zeitung, No. 843, November 24, 1922.

128 Freymuth, "Fechenbach-Feststellungen für die Geschichte,"
loc. cit. , 370.

129 Cf. Hirschberg, "Der Fall Fechenbach, " loc. cit. , 54-55.

130 Cf. Stampfer, Die ersten vierzehn Jahre der deutschen Republik, 318.

131 An admirable discussion of this particular dilemma of the republic is contained in Watkins, Failure of Constitutional
Emergency Powers, chap. iv. Watkins also demonstrates
convincingly that by taking stern measures against the left the
government mitigated the dangers from the right by taking the
wind out of the latter's sails.

132 Verordnung des Reichspräsidenten zur Wiederherstellung der
öffentlichen Sicherheit und Ordnung vom 10. August 1923 auf
Grund des Artikels 48, RGBl, 768. This decree dealt exclusively with the press, which apparently was considered the
major disturbing factor in the tense situation. The date of
issuance was the day when a general strike was declared in
Berlin.

133 Sten. Ber. , CCCLXI, 11887.

134 Ibid. , 11888.

135 Verordnung des Reichspräsidenten auf Grund des Artikel 48 Abs. 2 der Reichsverfassung betreffend die zur Wiederherstellung der öffentlichen Sicherheit und Ordnung für das Reichsgebiet nötigen Massnahmen vom 26. September 1923, RGBl, 905.

136 Verordnung über die Abänderung des bestehenden Ausnahmezustandes vom 23. Dezember 1923, RGBl, 1924, p. 8.

137 Cf. Watkins, Failure of Constitutional Emergency Powers, 40; Representative Breitscheid (SPD), Sten. Ber., CCLXI, 11953.

138 The number was given as between 25 and 30 by Representative G. Ledebour (USPD). Sten. Ber., CCCLXI, 12025.

139 Statement by Representative Breitscheid (SPD), ibid., 11953. The censorship blackout with reference to news about the Küstrin incident was confirmed by the minister of the army, Otto Gessler, who defended it as necessary to ensure the victory of the government. Ibid., 12017.

140 This term was used by the Frankfurter Zeitung, No. 491, July 6, 1923, in analogy to Bismarck's Anti-Socialist Act of 1878 suppressing the Socialist party.

141 Cf. discussion in the Reichstag of July 5, 1923, as reported in Frankfurter Zeitung, No. 491, July 6, 1923. Only in exceptional cases and only when the National-Socialists clashed with the Bavarian government was their organ, Voelkischer Beobachter, suppressed.

142 Frankfurter Zeitung, No. 741, October 6, 1923.

143 Ibid.

144 Frankfurter Zeitung, No. 795, October 26, 1923.

145 Ibid., No. 743, October 7, 1923.

146 Watkins, Failure of Constitutional Emergency Powers, chap. iv.

147 This situation was subject of complaint by the minister-president of Saxony in the "politische Aussprache" in the Reichstag of November 22, 1923. Sten. Ber., CCCLXI, 12221. He relayed that army district headquarters would refuse to enforce prohibition orders against Nationalist newspapers issued by Saxonian police authorities.

148 Representative K. Rosenfeld (SPD), citing substantial evidence, asserted in the Reichstag that the Communist press was hardly in existence and that even the SPD press was being suppressed to a considerable degree. His statement may have overdramatized the actual situation. Yet, it did not elicit protests from the government. Cf. ibid., 12267.

149 Entscheidungen des Reichsgerichts in Strafsachen, LVII, 209 ff.

150 Cf. Conrad, "Ein grundlegendes Urteil des Staatsgerichtshofs zum Schutz der Republik, " Deutsche Juristen-Zeitung, XXVIII (1923), 298-99. This decision confirmed prohibitions of National-Socialist papers.

151 Decision of June 2, 1923, cited in Juristische Wochenschrift, LIII (1924), 101.

152 Decision of February 9, 1924, cited ibid., 1777.

153 Decision of the Schöffengericht Berlin-Mitte of July 15, 1923, as cited in Frankfurter Zeitung, No. 517, July 16, 1923.

154 Cf. ibid., No. 506, July 12, 1923.

155 Cf. Watkins, Failure of Constitutional Emergency Powers, 47.

156 So for example A. J. Berlau, The German Social Democratic Party, 1914-1921 (New York: Columbia University Press, 1949), 9.

CHAPTER IV

1 Verordnung des Reichspräsidenten über die Aufhebung des militärischen Ausnahmezustandes und die Abwehr staatsfeindlicher Bestrebungen vom 28. Februar 1924, RGBl I, p. 153.

2 This condition, in its vagueness, somewhat resembled the rule of martial law in common-law countries inasmuch as review power over administrative acts was given to the Court of State. This arrangement forms a striking contrast to the decrees and law for the protection of the republic, which had established fairly objective criteria reducing as far as possible the discretion of an untrustworthy judiciary.

3 Verordnung des Reichspräsidenten auf Grund des Artikels 48
   Abs. 2 der Reichsverfassung zur weiteren Ergänzung der
   Verordnung vom 28. Februar 1924 über die Aufhebung des
   militärischen Ausnahmezustandes und die Abwehr
   staatsfeindlicher Bestrebungen. Vom 17. Juni 1924, RGBl I,
   p. 655.

4 Cf. Report to the Reichstag by Dr. W. Frick, rapporteur of the
   judiciary committee, Sten. Ber., CCCLXXXI, 711.

5 Ibid.

6 Cf. Rosenberg, History of the German Republic, 245-47.

7 Cf. Representative Koenen, Sten. Ber., CCCLXXXV, 1216. He
   lists specifically five Communist newspapers which were prohibited at that time for periods ranging from five to eight days.
   Since his statement was not contradicted by representatives of
   the government, it can probably be accepted as essentially
   correct.

8 Ibid., 1217.

9 Ibid., 1227.

10 Representative Crispien (SPD) cited the Rote Fahne of March 15
   as follows:
        "Gewalt geht vor Recht" — nun denn, wohlan!
        Einst kommt der Tag, da séid Ihr dran:
        Zehne für einen!

11 Sten. Ber., CCCXC, 7309.

12 Cf. Representative Rosenberg, ibid., 7296-7300. See also Representative Rosenfeld, ibid., 7655-56. See furthermore A.
   Rosenberg, History of the German Republic, 246; and E. J.
   Gumbel, Verräter verfallen der Fehme (Berlin: Malik-Verlag, 1929), passim.

13 Gesetz zur Abänderung des Gesetzes zum Schutz der Republik.
   Vom 8. Juli 1926, RGBl I, p. 397.

14 Sten. Ber., Drucksache, CCCXCIII, No. 3382.

15 Gesetz zur Verlängerung des Gesetzes zum Schutz der Republik.
   Vom 2. Juni 1927, RGBl I, p. 125.

16 Decision of the Court of State of May 15, 1924, cited in Juristische Wochenschrift, LIV (1925), 61-62.

[17] Amtsgericht Berlin-Mitte, referred to by A. Oborniker, "Schutz der Republik," Die Justiz, I (1926), 514-19.

[18] Cases of this nature are cited in Juristische Wochenschrift, LVII (1928), 816-17; LV (1926), 2755-56, 1199-1200; LVI (1927), 2703.

[19] StGB, sections 85 and 86. The German law distinguishes between "high treason" (Hochverrat) and "treason against the country" (Landesverrat). The former included activities aimed at the overthrow of the existing order through violent action from within while the latter referred to activities designed to expose the state to international dangers.

[20] Cf. A. Wegner, "Über Hochverrat," Die Justiz, III (1927), No. 2, p. 145.

[21] "Arbeiterschaft und Polizei," Sächsische Arbeiterzeitung, September 14, 1926. The case is cited by A. Oborniker, "Zur Hochverratspraxis des Reichsgerichts," Die Justiz, III (1928), No. 3, pp. 279-84.

[22] Decision of the Reichsgericht of February 5, 1927 (14 a J 99/25), cited in Juristische Wochenschrift, LVI (1927), 2003-2005. The case is discussed by Reichsgerichtsrat a. D. Conrad, "Vorbereitung des Hochverrats durch Verbreitung von Druckschriften. 'Literarischer Hochverrat'?" Deutsche Juristen-Zeitung, XXXII (1927), 800-803. See also Wegner, "Über Hochverrat," loc. cit.

[23] Examples are the Reimann, Schälicke, and Härzer cases decided in February and March, 1927, cited by W. Heine, "Die Buchhändler- und Druckerprozesse vor dem Reichsgericht," Die Justiz, II (1927), No. 4, pp. 350-65.

[24] Ibid. See also Häntzschel, "Das Recht der freien Meinungsäusserung," in Anschütz and Thoma (eds.), Handbuch des Deutschen Staatsrechts, II, 662, n. No. 26.

[25] Cf. A. Apfel, Behind the Scenes of German Justice. Reminiscences of a German Barrister 1882-1933 (London: John Lane, The Bodley Head Ltd., 1935), 114.

[26] Cf. Friedensburg, Die Weimarer Republik, 194.

[27] Cf. ibid., 196-98.

28 An impressive statistical survey is given by E. J. Gumbel,
"Landesverratsstatistik," Die Justiz, III (1928), No. 4,
passim. The author finds that the number of such prosecutions during the period under consideration had risen to thirty-
three times that of the prewar years.

29 Ibid., passim. See also G. Radbruch, "Der Landesverrat im
Strafgesetzentwurf," Die Justiz, III (1927), No. 2, pp. 103-
10.

30 H. Kantorowicz, "Der Landesverrat im deutschen Strafrecht,"
Die Justiz, II (1926), No. 1, pp. 92-102.

31 The pertinent facts had been published in the minutes of the
312th session of the budgetary committee of the Reichstag of
February 3, 1928, cited in Die Justiz, VII (1932), 198-99.
The case is discussed by Apfel, Behind the Scenes of German
Justice, 94-110. See also W. Karsch, "Carl von Ossietzky,"
Aufbau, Kulturpolitische Monatsschrift, I, No. 3, 219-24.

32 The Weltbühne incident was made subject of an interpellation
by the SPD in the Reichstag. See Die Justiz, VIII (1932),
198-99. Die Justiz also remarks that similar information had
been published by the Hamburger Nachrichten, which was not
prosecuted.

33 Entscheidungen des Reichsgerichts in Strafsachen, LXII, 65
ff. The case is discussed fully by L. Schücking, "Landesverrat und Friedensvertrag," Die Justiz, III (1928), Nos. 5/6,
pp. 509-16.

34 Kantorowicz, "Der Landesverrat im deutschen Strafrecht,"
loc. cit., 98.

35 Gumbel, "Landesverratsstatistik," loc. cit., passim.

36 E. J. Gumbel, "'Landesverrat' im Strafgesetzentwurf," Die
Menschenrechte. Organ der Liga für Menschenrechte, III
(1928), Nos. 9/10.

37 Gumbel, "Landesverratsstatistik," loc. cit., passim.

38 Ibid. The author points out that in the case of no other delict
was the proportion of initiated proceedings to those actually
carried through as abnormal as for that of Landesverrat
committed by the press.

39 Ibid., 262.

40 Cf. Löwenthal, "Der Landesverrat im Strafgesetzentwurf,"
Die Justiz, III (1927), No. 2, p. 120; also Gumbel,
"'Landesverrat' im Strafgesetzentwurf," loc. cit.; Radbruch, "Der Landesverrat im Strafgesetzentwurf," loc. cit.,
103-10.

41 This theme is ably discussed by H. Mayer, "Der strafrechtliche
Schutz des Staates," Süddeutsche Juristenzeitung, 1950, 247
ff.

CHAPTER V

1 Cf. Flechtheim, Die Kommunistische Partei Deutschlands in
der Weimarer Republik, 150.

2 Cf. Rosenberg, History of the German Republic, 289; Stampfer,
Die ersten vierzehn Jahre der deutschen Republik, 537;
Flechtheim, Die Kommunistische Partei Deutschlands in der
Weimarer Republik, chapter iv, passim; Friedensburg, Die
Weimarer Republik, 205.

3 Flechtheim, Die Kommunistische Partei Deutschlands in der
Weimarer Republik, 155.

4 Sten.Ber., CDXXV, 2743-47, 2919, 3077.

5 Representative Maslowski, ibid., 2748-49.

6 Ibid., 2916-17.

7 For an able discussion of this problem, see K. Loewenstein,
"Legislative Control of Political Extremism in European
Democracies," 38 Columbia Law Review (1938), 601-602.

8 Cf. Watkins, Failure of Constitutional Emergency Powers, 58.

9 Gesetz zum Schutz der Republik. Vom 25. März 1930, RGBl I,
91.

10 Statement by Karl Severing, Sten. Ber., CDXXVII, 4418.

11 Cf. Flechtheim, Die Kommunistische Partei Deutschlands in
der Weimarer Republik, chapter iv, passim.

[12]

Erbe, "Das neue Gesetz zum Schutz der Republik, " Deutsche
Juristen-Zeitung, XXXV (1930), No. 7, passim.

[13]

Derision, according to a declaration of the ministry of the interior and agreed to by the Reichstag committee, was to be
interpreted as a designation of the republican form of government as one afflicted with a moral defect or otherwise unworthy of the respect of the citizens. See, R. Lehmann,
"Das neue Gesetz zum Schutz der Republik, " Juristische
Wochenschrift, LIX (1930), Nos. 16 and 17.

[14]

This protection was not intended for the benefit of the persons
of ministers, but rather for the protection of the office. Cf.
secretary of state in the ministry of the interior, E. Zweigert,
Sten. Ber. , CDXXVII, 4461. K. Scheidemann, Die Neutralität des Staates gegenüber der Tagespresse (Diss. Handels-
hochschule, Berlin, 1933), 99, complains that the Reichsgericht did not establish the fact of an offense in cases where
a National-Socialist minister was libeled by the leftist press.
Actually, the position of the court was quite logical since
vilification or derision of a National-Socialist minister could
not possibly lower the prestige of the republic.

[15]

See debates of the Reichstag of February 9, 1931, concerning
amendment of the Press Law of 1874, Sten. Ber. , CDXLIV,
828-52. Early in 1931 the Press Law was amended to the
effect that nobody who could not be prosecuted or could be
prosecuted only with special permission could sign as responsible editor of a newspaper or periodical. Gesetz zur Abänderung des Reichsgesetzes über die Presse vom 7. Mai 1874.
Vom 4. März 1931, RGBl I, 29.

[16]

See statement of Representative Sollmann (SPD), Sten. Ber. ,
CDXLV, 1602-03.

[17]

Verordnung des Reichspräsidenten zur Bekämpfung politischer
Ausschreitungen. Vom 28. Marz 1931, RGBl I, 79.

[18]

Cf. K. Häntzschel, "Die neue Pressenotverordnung, " Juristische
Wochenschrift, LX (1931), 2077-79, 2424-25.

[19]

Zweite Verordnung des Reichspräsidenten zur Bekämpfung
politischer Ausschreitungen. Vom 17. Juli 1931, RGBl I,
371.

[20]

Cf. K. Häntzschel, "Die neue Pressenotverordnung, " loc. cit. ,
2077-79.

21 Ibid.

22 von Karger, "Wirtschaftsnot und Notgesetzgebung," Deutsche
    Juristen-Zeitung, XXXVI (1931), Nos. 17 and 18, pp. 1149-
    51.

23 The declaration appeared in the Berlin papers on August 8,
    1931, that is, one day before the voting.

24 Cf. M. Alsberg, "Zeitungsverbote," Zeitungswissenschaft
    (1932), Heft 6, p. 331; Häntzschel, "Die neue Pressenover-
    ordnung," loc. cit., 2077-79; F. Rummel, Die rechtliche
    Freiheit der Presse im liberalen und national-sozialistischen
    deutschen Staat (Diss. Göttingen, 1935), 36; Albrecht Dittmar,
    Die Beschrankungen der Pressfreiheit durch die Notverord-
    nungen des Reichspräsidenten (Diss. Erlangen, 1933), 26-28.

25 The Reichsgericht held that suppressions were preventive ad-
    ministrative acts, that this fact was manifested by the diver-
    gence of its procedure from criminal procedure, and that the
    purpose of the suppression was to prevent further publication
    of a newspaper which had proved harmful to the public interest.
    See decision of August 24, 1931, cited by Klimmer, "Verbote
    periodischer Druckschriften und Uniformverbote. Ein kurzer
    Überblick über die gesetzlichen Bestimmungen und die Recht-
    sprechung des 4. Strafsenats des Reichsgerichts," Leipziger
    Zeitschrift fur Deutsches Recht, XXVI (1932), 145-46. This
    view is not very convincing. Actually, it seems that these
    suppressions were in substance criminal law applied by ad-
    ministrative agencies.

26 Cf. Häntzschel, "Die neue Pressenotverordnung," loc. cit.,
    2077-79.

27 Verordnung des Reichspräsidenten zur Änderung der zweiten
    Verordnung zur Bekämpfung politischer Ausschreitungen.
    Vom 10. August 1931, RGBl I, 435; and Ausführungen und
    Richtlinien zur Handhabung der Verordnungen vom 28. März,
    17. Juli, 10. August 1931 des Reichsministers des Innern.
    Vom 10. August 1931, RGBl I, 436.

28 Dritte Verordnung des Reichspräsidenten zur Sicherung von
    Wirtschaft und Finanzen und zur Bekämpfung politischer
    Ausschreitüngen. Vom 6. Oktober 1931, RGBl I, 537 ff.

29 Hoche, "Dritte Verordnung des Reichspräsidenten zur
    Sicherung von Wirtschaft und Finanzen und zur Bekämpfung
    politischer Ausschreitungen," Deutsche Juristen-Zeitung,

XXXVI (1931), No. 20, pp. 1277-82.

30
Ibid.

31
The Protection Law and the earlier decrees had made prohibitions applicable also to Kopfblätter, that is, newspapers having identical contents but appearing under different names,
and to any new publication which was materially the suppressed newspaper in disguise.

32
Vierte Verordnung des Reichspräsidenten zur Sicherung von
Wirtschaft und Finanzen und zum Schutze des inneren
Friedens. Vom 8. Dezember 1931, RGBl I, 699 ff., Part
VIII.

33 * * * "Das Verbot der 'Kölnischen Volkszeitung' und des 'Vorwärts,'" Die Justiz, VII (1932), Nos. 10 and 11, pp. 482-96.

34
Watkins, Failure of Constitutional Emergency Powers, chapter
ix, passim.

35 Verordnung des Reichspräsidenten gegen politische Ausschreitungen. Vom 14. Juni 1932, RGBl I, 297.

36 Restrictions on posters, pamphlets, and handbills were reintro-
duced through the Zweite Verordnung des Reichsprasidenten
gegen politische Ausschreitungen. Vom 28. Juni 1932, RGBl
I, 339.

37
Cf. Th. Luddecke, Die Tageszeitung als Mittel der Staatsführung
(Hamburg: Hanseatische Verlagsanstalt, 1933), 150. The
fact that the government confined itself in actual practice to
official responses and only rarely resorted to positive official
declarations is interpreted by the author as an indication that
the government's will to restrict itself to the defensive pre-
dominated over its will to go over to the offensive.

38
Verordnung der Reichspräsidenten zur Erhaltung des inneren
Friedens. Vom 19. Dezember 1932, RGBl I, 548.

39
Klimmer, "Verbote periodischer Druckschriften und Uniformverbote ...," loc. cit., gives an extensive survey of the
cases affecting the press and decided by the Reichsgericht.

40
Franz Neumann, Das gesamte Pressenotrecht vom 4. Februar
1933. Systematischer Kommentar (Berlin: Verlag J. H. W.
Dietz Nachf. G. m. b. H., 1933), 43.

41
Arian and Oesterle, "Der Begriff der Gefährdung der öffent-
lichen Sicherheit und Ordnung bei Pressverboten, " Die
Justiz, V (1932), No. 4, 190.

42
Alsberg, "Zeitungsverbote," loc. cit., 332.

43
Numerous decisions substantiating these observations are
quoted by ibid., 333-35.

44 * * * "Das Verbot der 'Kölnischen Volkszeitung' und des
'Vorwärts,'" loc. cit., 482. See also the cases cited by
Alsberg, "Zeitungsverbote," loc. cit., and W. Heine,
"Staatsgerichtshof und Reichsgericht über das Hessische
Manifest," Die Justiz, VII (1932), No. 4, pp. 154-66.

45
Cf. Arian and Oesterle, "Der Begriff der Gefährdung der
öffentlichen Sicherheit und Ordnung bei Pressverboten,"
loc. cit.

46 * * * "Calumniare audacter! Neuer Gebrauch eines alten
Rezeptes," Die Justiz, VIII (1932), Nos. 2 and 3, p. 106.

47
Cf. decision of the Oberlandesgericht Jena of October 16, 1930,
cited in Juristische Wochenschrift, LX (1931), 80-81.

48
For decisions of the Reichsgericht illustrating these generaliza-
tions, see Klimmer, "Verbote periodischer Druckschriften
und Uniformverbote.....," loc. cit.

49
Cf. ibid.

50
Cf. ibid.

51
The truce took place on June 14, 1932. Cf. Stampfer, Die
ersten vierzehn Jahre der deutschen Republik, 628-29.

52
These cases are fully discussed by * * *, "Das Verbot der
'Kölnischen Volkszeitung' und des 'Vorwärts,'" loc. cit.,
482-96.

53
The following statements are a few random examples of remarks which the Supreme Court considered violations of
the press regulations: "The program of the government
is counter-revolutionary"; "Government officials are
being promoted for party political reasons"; "Ministers
are making their official decisions on the basis of instruc-
tions from their party superiors." Cf. Neumann, Das
gesamte Pressenotrecht vom 4. Februar 1933, 59-60.

[54] Alsberg, "Zeitungsverbote," loc. cit., 335.

[55] The brevity of the Schleicher regime does not permit any general observations concerning its actions in relation to the press. The one emergency decree issued by it with reference to the press has been discussed before.

CHAPTER VI

[1] This sentiment had been summed up by Adolf Stoecker as early as 1878, when he thundered in the "Eiskeller" speech at the Social Democrats: "You hate your Fatherland. ... to hate the Fatherland that is like hating your mother!" Quoted by L. L. Snyder, From Bismarck to Hitler. The Background of Modern German Nationalism (Williamsport, Pa.: The Bayard Press, 1935).

[2] Cf. Riesman, "Democracy and Defamation....," loc. cit., 1095-1100; Loewenstein, "Legislative Control of Political Extremism in European Democracies," loc. cit., 601-602; Friedensburg, Die Weimarer Republik, 208-20.

[3] Cf. Watkins, Failure of Constitutional Emergency Powers, chapter viii. He gives an excellent account of the legislative paralysis which pervaded the last years of the republic.

[4] * * * , "Calumniare audacter!....," loc. cit., 121.

[5] Cf. Loewenstein, "Legislative Control of Political Extremism in European Democracies, loc. cit., 595, n. 14.

[6] Cf. Alsberg, " Zeitungsverbote," loc. cit., 336-37.

[7] Cf. Arnold Brecht, Federalism and Regionalism in Germany. The Division of Prussia (New York: Oxford University Press, 1945), chapter vi; Rupert Emerson, State and Sovereignty in Modern Germany (New Haven: Yale University Press, 1928), chapter iii.

[8] Loewenstein, "Government and Politics in Germany," in Shotwell, Governments of Continental Europe, 340.

[9] For an excellent elaboration of this theme, see Mayer, "Der strafrechtliche Schutz des Staates," loc. cit., 247-55.

[10] Cf. Preuss, Deutschlands Republikanische Reichsverfassung, 89-91.

INDEX

145

LOUISIANA STATE UNIVERSITY STUDIES

Social Science Series

1. Postell, William Dosite, The Health of Slaves on Southern Plantations, 1951; $3.00 -- Out of Print

2. West, Robert C., Colonial Placer Mining in Colombia, 1952; $3.00

3. Richardson, W.C., Stephen Vaughan: Financial Agent of Henry VIII, 1953; $1.50.

Humanities Series

1. Hammer, Carl, Jr. (ed.), Goethe After Two Centuries, 1952; $2.50

2. Hammer, Carl, Jr., Longfellow's "Golden Legend" and Goethe's "Faust," 1952; $0.50

3. Krumpelmann, John T., Mark Twain and the German Language, 1953; $0.50

4. Uhler, John Earle, Morley's Canzonets for Two Voices, 1954; $2.50

5. Emerson, Everett H., John T. Krumpelmann, Foster Provost, H. B. Woolf, Contributions to the Humanities, 1954; $2.00

Biological Science Series

1. Dalquest, Walter W., Mammals of the Mexican State of San Luis Potosi, 1953; $3.50

2. Cochran, Fred D., Cytogenetic Studies of the Species Hybrid Allium fistulosum x Allium ascalonicum and Its Backcross Progenies, 1953; $2.00

3. Edgerton, Claude W., Sugarcane and Its Diseases, 1955; $5.00

Physical Science Series

1. Howe, Henry V., Handbook of Ostracod Taxonomy, 1955; $5.00